Writing across the curriculum

Year 3

Shelagh Moore and Sylvia Morgan

Shelagh Moore is a teacher with experience in primary, secondary and further education. She is currently working as a writer and trainer after over 20 enjoyable years in schools as a classroom teacher and in various management roles. She is happy to be contacted about her writing and to visit schools if requested.

Sylvia Morgan is an experienced primary school teacher. She has a long-term interest in language development and children with special needs. She has experience of developing the primary history curriculum in her own school and in developing workable strategies for assessment and testing.

Contents

		Page No
Introduction		3
Chapter 1: Recount writing	Unit 1 – Religious Education (Life of Jesus)	4
	Unit 2 – History (World War II)	14
Chapter 2: Report writing	Unit 1 – Geography (Local area)	25
	Unit 2 – History (Tudors)	36
Chapter 3: Instruction writing	Unit 1 – Music (Rhythmic patterns)	46
	Unit 2 – Design and Technology (Photo frames)	56
Chapter 4: Explanation writing	Unit 1 – Science (Teeth)	64
	Unit 2 – Citizenship (People who help us)	76
Chapter 5: Letter writing	Unit 1 – Geography (Weather)	83
	Unit 2 – Citizenship (Respect for property)	92

Published by
Hopscotch Educational Publishing Ltd
Unit 2
The Old Brushworks
56 Pickwick Road
Corsham
Wiltshire
SN13 9BX

01249 701701

© 2004 Hopscotch Educational Publishing

Written by Shelagh Moore and Sylvia Morgan
Series design by Blade Communications
Cover illustration by Susan Hutchison
Illustrated by Tim Hutchinson
Printed by Colorman (Ireland) Ltd

ISBN 1-904307-34-5

Shelagh Moore and Sylvia Morgan hereby assert their moral right to be identified as the authors of this work in accordance with the Copyright, Designs and Patents Act, 1988.

All rights reserved. This book is sold subject to the condition that it shall not, by way of trade or otherwise, be lent, hired out or otherwise circulated without the publisher's prior consent in any form of binding or cover other than that in which it is published and without a similar condition, including this condition, being imposed upon the subsequent purchaser.

No part of this publication may be reproduced, stored in a retrieval system, or transmitted, in any form or by any means, electronic, mechanical, photocopying, recording or otherwise, without the prior permission of the publisher, except where photocopying for educational purposes within the school or other educational establishment that has purchased this book is expressly permitted in the text.

Every effort has been made to trace the owners of copyright of material in this book and the publisher apologises for any inadvertent omissions. Any persons claiming copyright for any material should contact the publisher who will be happy to pay the permission fees agreed between them and who will amend the information in this book on any subsequent reprint.

▶ Writing Across the Curriculum   YEAR 3

Introduction

About the series

Writing Across the Curriculum is a series of books aimed at developing and enriching the writing skills of children at Key Stage 2. Matched to the National Literacy Strategy's *Framework for Teaching* and the QCA's Schemes of Work, each book contains comprehensive lesson plans in two different subject areas for recount, report, instruction, explanation, persuasion, letter (in Year 3) and discussion (in Year 6) writing.

There are four books in the series: Year 3, Year 4, Year 5 and Year 6.

Each book aims to:

- support teachers by providing detailed lesson plans on how to incorporate the teaching of writing skills within different subject areas;
- develop teachers' confidence in using modelled writing sessions by providing example scripts that the teachers can use or adapt;
- reduce teachers' preparation time through the provision of photocopiable resources;
- develop and enhance children's writing skills through stimulating and purposeful activities;
- encourage children's enjoyment of writing.

About each book

Each book is divided into separate chapters for each writing genre. Each chapter contains:

- an introductory page of teachers' notes that outline the key structural and linguistic features and guidelines on the teaching and progression of that particular writing genre;
- two units of work, each on a different subject area.

Each unit of work is divided into four lesson plans that can be carried out over a period of time. These lessons are called:

'Switching on' – introduces the concepts;

'Revving up' – develops the concepts;

'Taking off' – instigates the planning stage of the writing;

'Flying solo' – encourages independent writing.

Each lesson plan is divided as follows:

- Learning objectives;
- Resources;
- What to do;
- Plenary.

Most lessons are supported by **photocopiable sheets**. Some of these sheets provide background information for the children and others provide support in the form of writing frames. Most lessons have an exemplar text that can be shared with the children. There is usually an annotated version of this text for the teacher. The annotated version points out the structural and linguistic features of the text. It should be noted, however, that only one example of each feature is provided and that the features are presented as a guide only.

Chapter 1

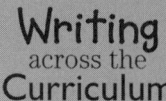

Recount writing

What is a recount text?

A recount is quite simply a retelling of an event. The retelling can be used to impart information or to entertain the reader. Recounts can be personal (from the point of view of someone who was there) or impersonal.

Structural features

- Usually begins with an introduction to orientate the reader. Often answers the questions 'who?', 'what?', 'when?', 'where?' and 'why?'
- Main body of text then retells the events in chronological order
- Ends with a conclusion that briefly summarises the text or comments on the event

Linguistic features

- Past tense
- First person (personal recounts) or third person (impersonal)
- Focuses on named individuals or participants
- Use of time connectives to aid chronological order (firstly, afterwards, meanwhile, subsequently, finally)
- Often contains interesting details to bring incidents alive to the reader

Examples of recount texts

- newspaper reports
- diary entries
- letters
- write-up of trips or activities
- autobiographies/biographies

Teaching recount writing

At first glance, recounts seem to be relatively straightforward; after all, children seem to get plenty of practice doing their 'news' writing at school! However, as with any retelling, it is easy for children to neglect to include vital pieces of information. The knowledge of the event is in the children's heads and it is our job, as teachers, to make sure that that knowledge is shared with the reader in order to make the event purposeful for them. Children tend to list events, as if on a timeline, but they need to include specific information and use relevant connectives so that the reader is able to have all the information needed to imagine themselves there.

Many children need a lot of support in organising the information chronologically. A flow chart is a useful tool to enable children to sequence events in the correct order. It also enables them to see where there are natural divisions for paragraphs. A word bank of time connectives could also prove useful.

Encourage the children to organise the planning of their recount by listing information under the headings: who, what, when, where and why. This will ensure they include all the vital information.

Recount writing – progression

Simple recounts are introduced in Key Stage 1 (Reception: T15; Year 1, Term 3: T20).

In **Year 3** children experiment with recounting the same event in a variety of ways, such as a story, a letter or a newspaper report (Term 3: T22).

In Year 4 children examine opening sentences that set scenes and capture interest and identify the key features of newspapers (Term 1: T18; T20). They write newspaper style reports (Term 1: T24). They learn to make short notes (Term 2: T21).

In Year 5 (Term 1: T21, T23, T24, T26) children learn to identify the features of recounted texts such as sports reports and diaries and to write recounts based on subject, topic or personal experiences for different audiences. They discuss the purpose of note taking and how this influences the nature of the notes made.

In Year 6 (Term 1: T11, T14, T15, T16; Term 3: T19, T22) children are reading to distinguish between biography and autobiography and are developing the skills of biographical and autobiographical writing in role. They review a range of text features and select the appropriate style and form to suit a specific purpose and audience.

Unit 1

Lesson focus
Religious Education Unit 3C – What do we know about Jesus?

Overall aim
To analyse the main features of a recount and to write a diary recount of Matthew meeting Jesus.

Religious Education emphasis
In this unit the children read different accounts of the life of Jesus and life in his time. They learn about Jesus as a person. They read and use information, discuss and question and use drama to communicate their learning. They use specialist terms where appropriate in their discussion and writing.

Literacy links
Year 3, Term 3: T3, T12, T17, T18, T22

About this unit
The children will learn about the sort of person Jesus was through reading Bible extracts and using other sources that may include videos, non-fiction texts and visitors (school chaplain/vicars) from the local Christian community. The children's understanding of writing recounts will be developed and consolidated by using the teacher's modelling as a guide and planning frames for support.

Switching on

Learning objectives
- To read and discuss the main points of a personal recount.
- To identify the linguistic features of a recount.
- To create a timeline of events.

Resources
- Sheets A and B (pages 10 and 11)
- A children's Bible
- Books/videos that show pictures of Jesus and what life was like in Palestine at that time

What to do
Tell the children that they are going to find out about the life of Jesus and his followers. Show them the Bible and explain that information on the teaching and life of Jesus is included in this book.

Ask them to tell you what they already know about Jesus. Write their answers on the board or a flip chart. You want them to tell you that Jesus started the Christian religion and that he told people about God. They may tell you that Christmas is when Christians celebrate the birth of Jesus and Easter is when Christians remember his death on the Cross.

Ask them to tell you what they think life was like during the time of Jesus. Share some of the books/videos that show pictures of the kind of clothes people wore and how they lived. You could divide the children into pairs or threes and provide them with some of the books. Ask them to look through and read any information that interests them. After about ten minutes, share what they have found out. Start a 'Jesus as a person' chart and add any relevant points to this.

Tell them that they are now going to find out about Matthew, a follower of Jesus, by reading a diary entry written by him. Share an enlarged version of Sheet A, which is based on Matthew 9, verses 9–13.

Ask them what they have learned from the reading. (Try to avoid using the word 'story' as this is an account of something that happened.) Write a summary of their comments on the board. What do they think of this account? Do they think it strange that someone should just leave his job and follow Jesus? Ask them to tell you

YEAR 3 Writing Across the Curriculum

how they think Matthew must have been feeling in order to just leave like he did. What clues in the text tell them this?

Explain that what they have just read is a personal recount – a recording of someone's thoughts and actions in their own words. Point out that it is written in the past tense and in the first person.

What do the children think are the important points in the account? You want them to tell you that Jesus visited Capernaum and that Matthew tells the reader about him. They should identify Matthew's job, what people of the time thought about tax collectors and how Matthew left his job to follow Jesus. Note their answers on the flip chart or board.

Show them a copy of Sheet B. Look at the top of the page together. Explain that recounts such as the diary entry usually contain information about 'who', 'where', 'when', 'what' and 'why'. Go through the questions together with them and ask them to give you answers that could be put in each box.

Explain that you now want them to record what happened in the account in the order that it happened. Tell them that they are going to retell the events later in their own words by writing their own recount.

Hand out copies of Sheet B and ask them to work in pairs to complete it. (The first event has been written in as an example.) You could prepare a word bank to help them with their writing. Identify the words they have used that are in it. Explain those they do not understand. (Possible words include: beliefs, Bible, Christians, crowd, disciples, followers, healer, miracle, preaching, salvation, tax collectors and teacher.)

As they complete Sheet B, walk around the class, discussing with them the choices they are making.

When they have written about three points, ask a confident pair to read their points out loud. Do the others agree with their order or would they have a different order?

Ask the children to check their sequence of incidents and complete the sheet.

Plenary

Ask the children to work in groups of four to make up a role play that re-enacts the events that happened, using Sheet B. Tell them that they should make sure that all the information about Jesus that Matthew mentions in his diary entry is included in their role play.

Ask them to act out their role play. At the end of the role plays ask the children what they have learned about Jesus. Add their responses to the 'Jesus as a person' chart.

Revving up

Learning objectives

■ To revise some of the features of a recount text.

■ To make a storyboard of events in sequence.

Resources

■ Sheets A, B and C (pages 10 to 12)

■ Notes from the previous lesson

What to do

Before this lesson, share some more extracts from the Bible about the life of Jesus in order to add more information to the 'Jesus as a person' chart.

Remind the children of their role plays at the end of the previous lesson. What had happened to Matthew? (You want them to tell you that Matthew had been called to follow Jesus.) What did Matthew tell them about Jesus? How did he tell them about Jesus? (You want them to remember that he wrote a personal recount in the form of a diary.) Discuss their answers, which should reflect the information on the 'Jesus as a person' chart.

Display an enlarged version of Sheet A and remind them about the use of the first person and past tense. Discuss the use of simple sentences and paragraphs for each new point in the text.

Writing across the Curriculum

Tell them that you now want them to imagine that they were part of the crowd who walked with Jesus into the town and saw Matthew joining Jesus. Tell them that you want them to do a storyboard of what happened, using their completed Sheet B and the notes from the previous lesson to help them. Say that in order to do this you want them to discuss in groups what happened. They should think about what it would have been like to be in the crowd. What would they have seen? Answers such as the type of people, what they were wearing and what the weather was like can be used. Ask them to think about how they would tell their friends at home what had happened.

Walk around the groups, saying out loud the points as they discuss them. Are there any words to explain and add to the word bank?

After the group discussion, provide them with a copy of Sheet C (which can be enlarged to A3) and ask them to draw a storyboard which shows what they saw happening. Give them about 20 minutes for this activity.

Pin the storyboards up around the classroom and let the children look at them. Do they think that the events are recorded in the correct chronological sequence? (They can number them to make sure that they use the correct sequence.)

Plenary

Ask the children to work in pairs and imagine that they are reporters and witnessed the day's events. Ask them to plan an interview that will tell others what happened when Matthew was called to Jesus. Tell them to use their storyboard to help them remember the sequence of events.

Choose some pairs to present their interview to the rest of the class. Do the audience agree that the interview accurately relates the events?

Taking off

Learning objective

■ To write the introduction to a diary recount.

Resources

■ Sheets A, C and D (pages 10, 12 and 13)

■ 'Jesus as a person' chart from previous lessons

What to do

Before this lesson it would be useful for the children to have read some more accounts of the life of Jesus and added more information to the 'Jesus as a person' chart. Christians from groups such as the Salvation Army or the local church could be invited into school to talk about how Jesus has influenced their lives – this may help the children understand why Matthew decided to follow Jesus. The children should be able to identify that Jesus cared about people and tried to help them as well as teaching them about God.

Tell the children that they are now going to use what they have found out in the previous lessons to plan and write their own personal diary recount, just like Matthew's. Explain that a personal recount is when they write about an incident from their own point of view.

Share an enlarged version of Sheet A. Ask them to remind you about the special features of a recount – it identifies 'who', 'where', 'when', 'what', and 'why'. It is written in the past tense and first person. It has paragraphs about events in chronological order.

Tell the children that you now want them to use their storyboards to write their own diary account of the meeting between Jesus and Matthew as if they were in the crowd that day watching everything that happened. They can use Sheet D to help them.

YEAR 3 Writing Across the Curriculum

Do some shared writing to model the beginning of the recount. You could use the script below. What you say as if talking to yourself is in italics; what you write is in bold.

Now, how should I begin? I am going to look at my storyboard to help me remember the order of the events that happened. I need to say where I was and why I was in town, so I could say: **I decided to go into town today to buy some fruit for my mother.** *Now what sort of day was it? What would I want to do if I was hot and thirsty?* (You could involve the children in helping you answer this question.) **It was a very hot day and I became very thirsty so I stopped at the well to get a drink.** *When I stopped to get a drink I could have been told about the visit, so I think I will write:* **When I was there someone told me that Jesus was visiting the town.** *Let me check back through that – have I written in the past tense and the first person? Yes. Now I need to say how the news made me feel.*

I could say that I was excited that Jesus was coming to our town. I could write: **When I heard that Jesus was coming to my town, I felt happy and excited.**

Ask the children if they can think of other words to describe how they might have felt and edit your writing to put in their choices. Ask them to check that your sentence makes sense. Is it in the past tense and the first person? What do they think you could put next? It is important to involve them in your writing as they could easily become distracted if they are not asked to contribute to the work in hand.

Ask them to write down what they think would make a good next sentence about what you did next. Listen to their suggestions and use the sentence that they think works best.

Hand out Sheet D and remind them that they can use this to help them plan their work. Say that you want them to write their own beginning to their diary recount (similar to how it was modelled with the class). Remind them that they have to imagine what it must have been like to be there that day. Walk around the class as they do this to check that they are using the first person and the past tense. Share good examples with the rest of the class.

Plenary

Ask the children to get into groups of three or four to share each other's beginnings. Can their friends suggest ways to improve them? Share good ideas with the rest of the class. Explain that they will be completing their recounts in the next lesson.

Flying solo

Learning objectives

■ To complete a diary recount.

Resource

■ Children's work from previous lessons

What to do

Remind the children about their work in the previous lesson. Tell them that they are now going to complete their diary recounts. Ask them to remind you about the things they need to remember when writing a recount. Remind them to use their storyboards to help them remember the correct sequence of events.

Explain that before they do this, you want to help them write a conclusion to their recounts.

Ask them what a conclusion is. (You want them to tell you that it is a way of ending their recount.) Tell them that you are going to model a conclusion for them to help them with their writing. You could use the script below as before. What you say as if to yourself is in italics; what you write is in bold.

You might begin by saying, *I think I will write about how the day ended. I will start by writing* **I heard Jesus tell Matthew to follow him. Matthew got up and left the custom house and went with Jesus.** Ask the children if they think what you have put is a good start to the conclusion. Say *What can I put next?*

Listen to their ideas and write a sentence that shows what your reaction was to Matthew leaving his work to follow Jesus. You can ask them to check that you have written the sentence in the past tense and in the first person.

Writing Across the Curriculum   YEAR 3

I am going to write my final sentences. I think I shall write:
What a strange day it has been! I have seen Jesus and heard him speak. As well as that, Matthew the tax collector has left his job. I wonder what will happen next?

Ask the children if they think what you have written ends the diary entry.

Then ask them to begin their own writing. They could work in pairs to support each other. Work with a group of children who need further support.

When they have completed their recounts, ask them to work with a response partner to check their work. You could write the following questions on the board for them to respond to:

- Is it clear that this is a diary entry?
- Is it written in the first person and the past tense?
- Is it written in sentences that start with capital letters?
- Is it clear what it is about?
- Does it tell you what happened?
- Does anything need changing?
- Are there any spellings to check?

Plenary

Read out a selection of the diary entries. Do they give the reader a good idea of what the day was like for the writer? Do we learn anything else that can be added to the 'Jesus as a person' chart?

The children could follow up these lessons by making a fact file about Jesus. It could include pictures and a list of facts learned about Jesus. The fact files could be displayed together with the diary entries.

Sheet A

Matthew was a tax collector who met Jesus. People didn't like Matthew because he was a tax collector – he was an outcast. He collected money from the people and gave it to the Romans. Because some tax collectors kept some of the money they had collected, the people disliked all tax collectors. Matthew had been a tax collector for a number of years and worked in the custom house in the city of Capernaum every day. Here is an entry in Matthew's diary:

Something amazing happened to me today – I met Jesus! I had heard about Him before. I had heard that He went around the country teaching people about God and how to please God. He healed the sick and preached to the people. People said it was good to hear his words. They said his preaching was unusual because He told people to love one another and to be kind and caring towards each other – and that's not easy!

I woke up early, feeling that today was going to be a special day. I looked out at the street and saw my neighbours going about their work. I got up and ate my breakfast of fruit and bread. I had a drink and dressed to go to work. The day was hot and the streets were busy. I walked through the market place to the custom house.

When one of the other tax collectors told me that Jesus was to be in Capernaum today I was very curious to see him but I was very sad because I had to work and I could not leave my room in the custom house. How I wanted to go and see this miracle worker!

At about noon, I was distracted from my work by the noise of a huge crowd outside. I looked up and caught a glimpse of Jesus as he walked past. He paused and looked at me. I felt that he knew all about me and that he cared about me. Not many people care about tax collectors I can tell you!

I heard the words 'Follow me,' so I got up and left the Custom House for the last time. I have become a follower of Jesus. Some people were unhappy that Jesus had called to me, a tax collector, because I am an outcast. Some people said that all tax collectors are bad because they keep some of the taxes they collect for themselves. But I am not like that! Jesus put them in their place. He said that he had come to call all outcasts. I felt calm and peaceful and knew that I had done the right thing. I know I have decided to follow someone who is a very special person.

I wonder what tomorrow will bring?

Writing Across the Curriculum

PHOTOCOPIABLE

Sheet B

Sequencing framework

Who? Who is the account about? Who else is mentioned?	When? When does the account take place?	Where? Where does the action take place?

What? What happens in the account?	Why? Why does the action take place?

Use the boxes below to put the events in the correct order that they happened.

The first one has been done for you.

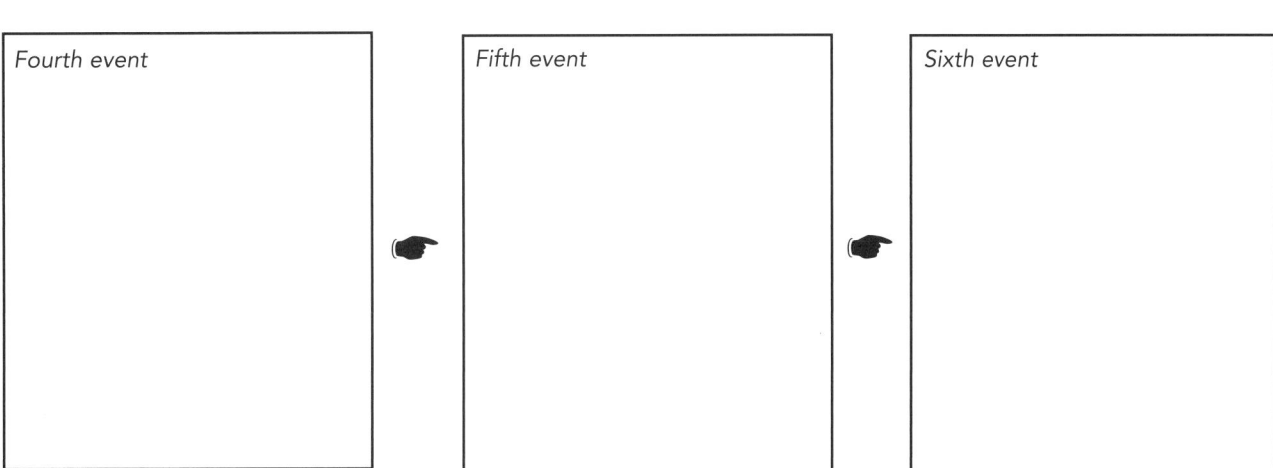

PHOTOCOPIABLE — Writing Across the Curriculum

Sheet C

Storyboard

Draw pictures to show the events in the order that they happened.

Think about the things you would have seen if you were in the crowd outside the custom house when Jesus passed it and called Matthew to follow Him.

What sort of day was it?   What were people doing?   What did you see?

Writing Across the Curriculum

PHOTOCOPIABLE

Sheet D

This is a diary entry by _____ written during the evening on the day Matthew the tax collector was called by Jesus.

Introduction

Say what sort of day it was and why you had decided to go and see Jesus. Tell what you knew about Him. Remember to write in the first person. Use the past tense. Write about three sentences.

Development

Using your storyboard as a guide to remind you, say who was there, what happened, how it happened and why you think it happened. Make sure the events you write about are in the correct order. Write about four sentences.

Conclusion

Explain what your reaction to the day's events was. What did you think of Matthew and Jesus when it was all over? Write your own views here. Say what it was like to see someone leave everything and follow Jesus. Write about three sentences.

Unit 2

Lesson focus
History Unit 9 – What was it like for evacuees in the Second World War?

Overall aim
To analyse the main features of a recount and to write a newspaper account of evacuation during World War II.

History emphasis
In this unit the children use information texts, videos, drama and first-hand accounts to gather information about the evacuation. They will be encouraged to ask questions about and give reasons for the evacuation. They will learn what it was like for young children to be taken from their families to spend time with strangers in places far away from where they lived.

Literacy links
Year 3, Term 3: T3, T17, T18, T22

About this unit
The children will learn about the evacuation of children during the Second World War from a range of sources that may include videos, first-hand accounts, drama and fiction as well as non-fiction texts. They will look at artefacts and contemporary reports and materials such as photographs and posters. They will write a newspaper-style recount of the evacuation. The teacher will model writing a recount text and the children will use a simple sequence planning line in order to help them both to sequence their understanding of events and to plan their writing.

Switching on

Learning objectives
- To read and discuss the main points of an impersonal recount.
- To identify the structural and linguistic features of a recount.
- To make a summary of text read.

Resources
- Sheets A, B and C (pages 19 to 21)
- A timeline with key dates of World War II from 1938 to 1945 (a 'washing line' with pegs and cards works well)
- Information books about World War II that include sections on the Blitz and evacuation

What to do
Before this lesson, the children should have already started to learn about the Second World War and the Blitz.

Reintroduce the history timeline, discussing key dates and events learned about so far. Ask the children to tell you what they know about the Blitz. Write key points on the board.

Introduce the word 'evacuee' to the children; ask them if they know what it means. Explain the term 'evacuated'. Tell them they are going to find out how and why children were evacuated during the war.

Read one or two short passages from a textbook or big book about evacuation to the children. Ask why they think it was necessary for children to be evacuated. Add key ideas to the board.

Show the children an enlarged version of Sheet B. Use the annotated version (Sheet A) as your guide. Tell them they are going to read a newspaper account of the evacuation of a brother and sister during the war. Explain that a newspaper report is actually a recount because it is telling us about something that has already happened. Tell them that you want them to read the text to learn about evacuation as well as learning about the special features of a recount text. Tell them that they will be writing their own recount later.

Share the text. Discuss any unfamiliar vocabulary. Ask them to tell you what the text is about. Who is the account about? What happens?

Ask the children to tell you what they notice about how the recount is written. You want them to notice the heading, layout and general features, such as the use of the past tense. Using Sheet A as your guide, annotate the text as you discuss each feature the children notice and then go on to point out and discuss all the other features on the sheet. You could comment on the following in particular:

- the meaning of the term 'impersonal';
- the use of the third person – 'he', 'she' and 'they' – not 'I', 'we' or 'you';
- the use of complete sentences;
- the use of paragraphs.

Discuss the use of headlines in newspaper reports and ask the children if they can invent a new headline for the recount. Write their ideas on the board.

Tell the children that you now want them to make a record of all the information contained in the text. Tell them that recount texts usually include information about 'who', 'what', 'where', 'when' and 'why' in relation to the event. Show them an enlarged version of Sheet C. Point out each of the boxes and explain that answering the questions will help them to work out what they have read. Model the answers in the first box for them.

Provide the children with their own copy of Sheet C. Ask them to work in pairs to complete it. Circulate around the class, sharing good ideas as you come across them.

Ask each pair to share their work with an adjacent pair. Tell them to check that they have included all the main points. Ask them to consider whether their answers will be exactly the same or different and why.

Plenary

Ask the children to tell you what they have learned about how a recount is written. Brainstorm their responses and write them as a bullet-pointed list on a flip chart to use as a recount writing guide for the classroom.

You are looking for the following types of answers: a recount is rather like writing news; it tells the reader about something that has happened; it is usually written in the past; it is written in the third person, which means the writer uses he, she and they, not we, you and I; it is usually written in chronological order; it is written in complete sentences; it is organised into paragraphs.

Revving up

Learning objectives

- To analyse the order of events in a recount.
- To make a record of the sequence of events in a recount.

Resources

- Sheets B and D (pages 20 and 22)

What to do

Prior to this session, read the children some stories about evacuees (such as the first chapters of *Carrie's War* by Nina Bawden or *My Story – Blitz, the Diary of Edie Benson* by Vince Cross).

Display an enlarged version of Sheet B. What do the children remember about the newspaper account? What can they remember about some of the features of a recount text? Share their ideas. Tell them that another important feature of a recount is that the events are told in the order they happened. Explain that you want them to look at the text again and make a summary of all the events that took place – in the order that they happened.

Show them Sheet D and explain that the sequence line is a bit like the history timeline and that it will help them sort out the time sequence of what happened in the account. Tell them that they can either write or draw pictures in each cloud shape to show what happened.

Writing across the Curriculum

Ask questions aimed at helping the children to see the sequence of events in the text, such as 'What happened first?', 'What happened last?', 'When did the children pack their cases?', 'Then what happened?', 'What happened at the station?', 'What happened when they boarded the train?' and so on.

Point out the first cloud shape on Sheet D and, working as a class, model the writing for it, for example:

> *Monday – Mrs Adams told May and John that they were going to be evacuated to Somerset.*

Ask for a suggestion for the last cloud and then for a few key points in between, referring back to the text as you go. The information contained in the paragraphs of the text could be split into more than one incident. For example, in paragraph 4 there could be three incidents:

1. They walked to the train station.
2. Officials gave them name labels.
3. They waited for the train.

Provide the children with their own copies of Sheets B and D and ask them to work in pairs to complete the sequence sheet. Ask them to reread the text and then decide which key events in the text to write or illustrate. Tell them they can use a marker pen to highlight sections and/or number the events to help them.

Give them time to complete the task and choose one group of children to work with to support. (One way of differentiating the activity would be to ask less able children to enter fewer points on the frame. You could prepare a simplified version of the sheet.)

Plenary

Ask the children to compare the writing timeline with the history timeline. How is it the same and how different? Emphasise the fact that both lines help the children put events/facts in the right sequence/order.

Ask the pairs of children to work with an adjacent pair. Tell each pair to check the other's work, making sure that most of the main points are included. Point out that the other pair's points may not necessarily be exactly the same as their own.

Ask some children to share their recount sequence line with the rest of the class.

Taking off

Learning objectives

- To find out about the evacuation of children during the Second World War.
- To plan a newspaper recount.

Resources

- Sheets D and E (pages 22 and 23)
- A collection of resources about evacuation

What to do

Prior to this session, it would be very helpful to build on the children's knowledge about evacuation by looking at a video or listening to a visitor who can provide a first-hand account. Share some contemporary accounts of evacuation with the children. Look at photos of children being evacuated and ask your children what they think was happening and how those children might have felt.

Tell them that they are going to do some research to find out what happened when the children were evacuated from the cities to the country. Show them the range of resources you have made available for them to use.

Say that you want them to make short notes about what they find out about evacuation and explain that they will use them later to write their own newspaper articles about evacuation. Tell them that you want them to find out about the following things:

- When the children were evacuated;
- Why they were evacuated;
- Who decided that they should go;
- How they were evacuated;

Writing Across the Curriculum   YEAR 3

- Where they went to;
- Who took them there;
- How they travelled there;
- What happened when they arrived.

Write these points on the board.

You could try the idea below to help the children do their research:

1. Divide them into pairs. Name one person 'A', the other 'B'.
2. Provide each pair with (a) suitable resource(s).
3. Tell them that all 'A' people are 'scribes' – they need a pencil and paper to record things.
4. Tell them that all 'B' people are 'communicators' – they need to remember things to tell others. (You may want to make sure you divide the pairs into children who are more suited to each type.)
5. Time them (say three minutes) to find out what they can about the topic from the resource(s) they are sharing.
6. After the time is up, tell all 'B' people to stand up and move on to sit with a different 'A' person.
7. When they meet their new person it is 'A''s job to read what they have already written to the new person. It is 'B''s job to tell 'A' what they have found out.
8. Continue changing every three minutes.

This is an excellent way to keep the children on task. It enables them to work with lots of different partners and provides each partner with a definite purpose. It is a great way of sharing and remembering facts and eliminates the problem of children taking different amounts of time to carry out their research.

When the children have completed their research, draw the class together and brainstorm a list of the main points that they have found out. Write these on a flip chart or whiteboard.

Tell them that you want them to use this information to write their own newspaper account about evacuation. Remind the children that the newspaper recount about May and John included information about 'who', 'when', 'where', 'why' and 'what'. Show them an enlarged version of Sheet E. Tell them that they can use this to plan their writing.

Look at the first question together. Ask them to invent some evacuees (or give the names of some real ones from their research) that their account could be about. Write their suggestions on the board. Do the same for the other questions.

Provide the children with their own copies of Sheet E to complete, using their own ideas. They could work in pairs to do this.

After a while, gather the class back together again. Remind them about the 'sequence sheet' they completed for the May and John account (Sheet D). Tell them that now they have planned their facts for their newspaper account they can use another copy of this sheet to plan the order of the events for their own recount. You could say: *'You will need to decide on a starting point for the recount; who can give me their ideas? You will also need to decide on an end point for your recount. For example, will your recount end when the children are on the train or when they arrive with the host family? Think about how much writing you plan to do for the middle of the account. Use the cloud shapes to help you.'*

The children could work in pairs again to complete Sheet D. Remind them that they should only write brief notes and that they can use pictures. Circulate around the class helping the children, reading out good ideas.

Plenary

Share the children's planning and sequence of events sheets. Do they feel confident that they now have enough information to write their newspaper recounts? Ask them to decide on a suitable headline for their recount, such as 'Sunshine School – Children Evacuated!' or 'Bomb Fears – Children Evacuated!' Write their ideas on the board.

Writing across the Curriculum

Flying solo

Learning objective
- To write a newspaper recount.

Resources
- Sheet F (page 24)
- Children's planning from previous lesson

What to do

Tell the children that they are now going to write their newspaper recount, using their planning and sequence sheets to help them.

Ask them to remind you of the special features of a newspaper recount text to make sure they know what to do.

Give them a short time to remind themselves of the facts they are going to use for their recount. They could work in pairs to look at their completed Sheet E. One child could read it to the other.

Provide each child with a copy of the writing frame (Sheet F). Explain that they will use this to help them write their recount. Start by looking at the writing frame as a whole; explain each section briefly, talking through the instructions with them. Remind them that the introduction tells the reader what the recount is going to be about, while the conclusion sums up what they have read.

Ask them to write in their headline. Then go through the introduction section with them and do some shared writing to model how the introduction could be written. Take care to show them how to link this section back to the appropriate section of Sheet E, using one pair of children's planning as an example.

Tell me who your recount is about. (Peter and Emily Green.) *What else do you know about them?* (They are a brother and sister aged 10 and 7 from Tooting in London.) *What happened?* (They were evacuated from their home to Kent.) *When did the event happen?* (Yesterday.) *Why did it happen?* (They were sent away to be safe from the bombing of London.)

Then start modelling the writing. You could use the script below. What you say, as if to yourself, is in italics; what you write is in bold.

Good. Now we have all the information, let's try putting it into sentences. I'm going to start with yesterday, so: **Yesterday, Peter and Emily Green, a brother and sister aged 10 and 7 from Tooting in London, were evacuated to Kent.** *I'm going to change the last sentence a bit to make it short and clear.* **They were sent away to escape the bombing of London.**

Have I written it all in the third person? Is it all written in the past tense?

Talk them through each point in this way, writing it on a whiteboard or enlarged version of the frame. Talk them through the punctuation as you go and think out loud about the choice of language you are using. When you have completed the introduction, read it out together.

Then ask the children to write their own introductions. Stop them after a while and share their introductions. Discuss the good points and ways of making improvements.

Ask the children to continue drafting their recount. Remind them that the vertical lines on Sheet D will help them to decide when to start new paragraphs/events. Sheet E will remind them of all the information they need.

While they are drafting, circulate and help with the writing process. When this is complete, the children could share their draft with a partner. You could write a list based on the recount checklist on page 9 to help them. Ask them to check that it makes sense and that it follows in reasonable time order.

Plenary

Ask the children to read their recount aloud to a new partner. Ask them to tell their partner one good thing about the recount and one thing that can be improved.

Sheet A

- name of newspaper and date
- introduction tells us 'who', 'when', 'where', 'what' and 'why'
- focus on named individuals
- third person (an impersonal recount)
- time connective
- past tense
- events told in chronological order
- set out in paragraphs
- headline
- photo to aid the reader's understanding
- caption
- conclusion

The Wandsworth Daily Echo

Wednesday, 12th June, 1940

JOHN AND MAY EVACUATED TO SAFETY!

JOHN ADAMS (10) and MAY ADAMS (8), a brother and sister from Chigwell Street, London, were amongst those children from Chigwell Primary School who were evacuated to Somerset yesterday.

It was on Monday that their mother, Mrs Alice Adams, had to break the sad news to them about their trip to Somerset. She said, "They were very upset, especially May, who spent the whole day crying and saying she wanted to stay here with me. I don't know how I'm going to bear being without them."

On Monday evening, along with all the other children from Chigwell Primary School, John and May packed their tiny suitcases. They were allowed to take only one favourite toy.

Early on Tuesday morning, Mrs Adams walked John and May to the railway station. On arrival, officials took their names and issued them with labels which were pinned to their clothes. There were over 100 other children waiting to be evacuated with them. John and May were very nervous waiting for the train; May

John and May say goodbye.

clutched her teddy bear and John tried to look brave and grown-up.

At 10 o'clock, the train came into the station and John and May said farewell to their mother. There were lots of tears and lots of hugs and kisses. The children all boarded the train and were guided to a seat by their teachers. They waved to their mothers as the train slowly moved out of the station, taking them to Taunton, safety and a whole new way of life.

Sheet B

The Wandsworth Daily Echo

Wednesday, 12th June,, 1940

JOHN AND MAY EVACUATED TO SAFETY!

JOHN ADAMS (10) and MAY ADAMS (8), a brother and sister from Chigwell Street, London, were amongst those children from Chigwell Primary School who were evacuated to Somerset yesterday.

It was on Monday that their mother, Mrs Alice Adams, had to break the sad news to them about their trip to Somerset. She said, "They were very upset, especially May, who spent the whole day crying and saying she wanted to stay here with me. I don't know how I'm going to bear being without them."

On Monday evening, along with all the other children from Chigwell Primary School, John and May packed their tiny suitcases. They were allowed to take only one favourite toy.

Early on Tuesday morning, Mrs Adams walked John and May to the railway station. On arrival, officials took their names and issued them with labels which were pinned to their clothes. There were over 100 other children waiting to be evacuated with them. John and May were very nervous waiting for the train; May

John and May say goodbye.

clutched her teddy bear and John tried to look brave and grown-up.

At 10 o'clock, the train came into the station and John and May said farewell to their mother. There were lots of tears and lots of hugs and kisses. The children all boarded the train and were guided to a seat by their teachers. They waved to their mothers as the train slowly moved out of the station, taking them to Taunton, safety and a whole new way of life.

Sheet C

Who is the recount about? Describe them.

When did it happen?

Where did it happen?

What happened?

Why did it happen?

Sheet D

You can picture plan or use notes.

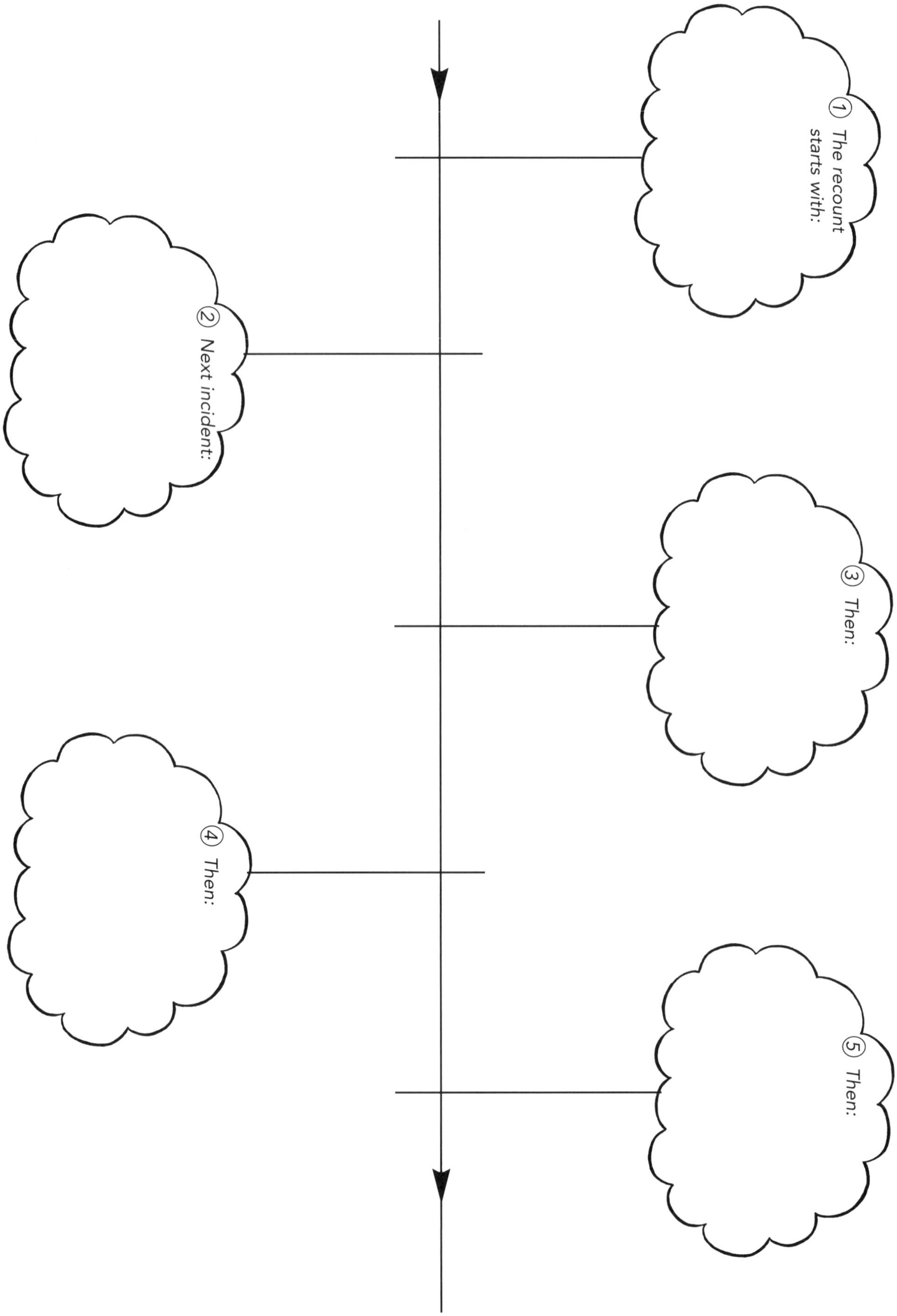

① The recount starts with:

② Next incident:

③ Then:

④ Then:

⑤ Then:

Sheet E

Who was evacuated? What were their names?

Who decided they should go?

Who took them?

Who travelled with them?

When were they evacuated?

Where did they have to go? How did they travel?

What happened when they were evacuated?

Why were they evacuated?

Sheet F

*Write your **headline** here. Make it bold and eye-catching.*

*Write your **introduction** here. Include information about **who**, **when**, **where**, **what** and **why**.*

*Do a **drawing** here. Write a **caption** to go with it.*

Write the rest of the recount here. Remember to write about the events in the order they happened.

*Write your **conclusion** here.*

Chapter 2

Writing across the Curriculum

Report writing

What is a report text?

A report is a non-chronological text written to describe or classify something. It brings together a set of related information and sorts it into paragraphs of closely connected facts. Reports can also be used to compare and contrast.

Structural features

- Usually begins with an introduction to orientate the reader. Tells us 'who', 'what', 'where' and 'when'
- Main body of text is organised into paragraphs describing particular aspects of the subject
- Ends with a conclusion that briefly summarises the text
- Non-chronological

Linguistic features

- Often written in the present tense (except for historical reports)
- Usually uses generic nouns and pronouns (such as people, cats, buildings) rather than specific ones
- Written in an impersonal third person style
- Factual writing often using technical words
- Language is used to describe and differentiate
- Linking words and phrases are used
- Occasional use of the passive

Examples of reports

- non-fiction books
- newspaper/magazine articles
- information leaflets, tourist guidebooks

Teaching report writing

Writing a non-chronological report is a bit like collecting shells on the beach in a bucket and then sorting them into piles of similar shells, discarding anything that is damaged or has been scooped up that isn't a shell!

Children need to learn to gather from research relevant information about the subject they are going to describe, sort the information into groups of facts that go together and then link them in a logical order, both within the paragraphs and between the paragraphs. They have to learn how to 'file' information into these paragraphs so that the reader can access the information easily and logically. Using subheadings for paragraphs can help children organise their information. They need to choose which information is most important to the reader and elaborate on it.

One of the difficulties for children is to be able to research the information they need without simply copying out (or printing out) passages from reference sources. They need to be taught how to select key words and phrases and use them in their own sentences.

Report writing - progression

Simple non-chronological reports are introduced in Key Stage 1 (Year 1, Term 2: T25; Year 2, Term 3: T21).

In **Year 3** children locate information in non fiction books using the text structures – contents, index, headings, subheadings, page numbers and bibliographies. They record information from texts and write simple non-chronological reports for a known audience (Term 1: T17, T18, T21, T22).

In Year 4 children identify different types of text and different features of non-fiction texts in print and IT (Term 1: T16, T17) and they write non-chronological reports, including the use of organisational devices (Term 1: T21).

In Year 5 (Term 1: T26; Term 2: T22) children learn to make notes for different purposes and to plan, compose, edit and refine short non-chronological texts.

In Year 6 (Term 1: T17; Term 3: T19, T22) children are moving onto writing non-chronological reports linked to other subjects. They review a range of text features and select the appropriate style and form to suit a specific purpose and audience.

Unit 1

Lesson focus
Geography Unit 6 – Investigating our local area

Overall aim
To write a report that describes the physical and human features of the local area.

Geography emphasis
This unit encourages the children to investigate their local area. They will describe the physical and human features of their location and use geographical language. They will use a range of sources, both primary and secondary.

Literacy links
Year 3, Term 1: T20, T22, S11, S12

About this unit
In this unit, the children will develop their ability to find and use information for a specific purpose. They will use first-hand observation, visual information (photos, maps) and written information (non-fiction texts).

They will answer key questions about how to report on the locality of their school.

Switching on

Learning objectives
- To identify the key features of a non-chronological report.
- To make notes.

Resources
- Sheets A, B, C and D (pages 32 to 35)

What to do
Tell the children they are going to read a report about a school and find out about its location. Explain that they are going to use the report to make notes.

Briefly revise the terms 'report' and 'making notes'. Ask them if they know what a report is. Use a flip chart to briefly outline their answers. Brainstorm what notes are and what they are used for. Use their ideas to write a note making guide on the board.

Share an enlarged copy of Sheet B with the children and ask them to tell you what it is about. Show them the map of the area described in the report (Sheet C) and ask them to find some of the places mentioned.

Explain the key features of a report by pointing out the following things (use Sheet A as your guide):

- it has an introduction that tells us what the report is about;
- it has a title and sometimes has subheadings;
- it is usually written in the present tense, third person;
- it contains facts;
- it is organised into paragraphs;
- it ends with a conclusion.

Ask the children to tell you if they notice any special words in the report. Identify any key words (look for subject words like 'location', 'facilities', 'situated', 'opposite', 'near', 'left' and 'right' – the language of place) that will help them to understand the main points in the paragraphs and circle them.

Read the report again (perhaps a child could read it) and ask the children to pick out the main points and underline them.

Using an enlarged version of Sheet D, show the children how they can use the wheel to help them to organise some notes. Ask them to identify any words that were circled and phrases that were underlined that belong in the inner oval on the wheel (the school). Repeat this for the other two ovals (near the school and further from the school).

Explain that using the wheel in this way has enabled them to organise the notes according to the three geographical areas mentioned in the report.

Tell them that they are now going to carry out the same note making task themselves. Cover up the enlarged class versions and provide them with their own copies of Sheets B and D. They could work in pairs to read the report together and pick out the key points. Ask them to underline the main points and circle the key words and then enter them on the wheel in note form in their own words.

Plenary

Ask the pairs of children to share their notes with another pair of children and compare their answers. Have they included all the important information? Did they find circling words and underlining phrases helpful?

Give the children a home task (or carry out a whole class excursion before the next lesson) to help lead into the next lesson. Ask them to use another copy of Sheet D to note what they see on their journey to and from school. Remind them what the headings mean – 'the school' means the area literally inside and outside the school fence. They need to note any human and physical features they see, such as pedestrian crossings, road signs, shops, streetlights, houses, grass verges, streams and so on. 'Near the school' means the area in the streets closest to the school. 'Further from the school' covers the outskirts of the village/town/city that the school is in. Ask them to list any human features such as shops and factories, open spaces such as parks and the road names and any physical features, such as hills, valleys, rivers, lakes, ponds and so on. Display their notes so that everyone can see the different observations they have made.

Revving up

Learning objectives

- To make notes.
- To use notes to organise and present ideas.
- To write the introduction to a report.

Resources

- Sheets A, B, C and D (pages 32 to 35)
- Aerial photographs, maps and books of own school and local area

What to do

Prior to this lesson, the children need to have completed a note making wheel (Sheet D) for their own local area, either as a homework task or as a whole class activity.

Ask the children to tell you what they can remember about Fir Tree Primary School. Show them the map (Sheet C) and the completed note making wheel from the previous lesson to remind them. Ask them to tell you briefly what is the same and what is different about the area surrounding Fir Tree School Primary and the area surrounding their own school.

Tell them that they are going to write their own report about the area surrounding their school, similar to the report they read about Fir Tree School. Ask them to tell you what they remember about the special features of a report. Use an enlarged version of Sheet A to revise each point.

Remind the children about the notes they made about their own local area. Tell them they are going to use these notes to help them write their report. Explain that they are also going to gather some more information by looking at maps, photos and books about the area.

Discuss the photographs and maps first to ensure understanding. Ask the children to pick out key features. Ask questions such as 'What can you see outside our school?', 'What is there at the end of the playground?' and 'What shop is next to…?' Locate their answers on the photos and maps. Discuss 'north' and 'south' and relate them to the photos and maps.

Divide the class into mixed ability groups and provide them with some aerial photos, maps and books. Ask them to use their note making wheel sheets and the resources to brainstorm information needed for their report.

At the end of this session, ask for a spokesperson from each group to read out their notes. Note their key points on the board.

Explain that you are now going to show them how to use the notes they have made to begin writing the report. Decide on an audience. It would be a good idea to pair up with a neighbouring school or class to have real recipients for the reports.

Model writing the introduction, along the following lines. What you say, as if to yourself, is in italics; what you write is in bold.

I am going to write a heading for my report. I think I will call it **The Location of** *(your school name)* **School**. *Can you think of any other titles that would explain what the report is about?'* Brainstorm some alternative ideas with the children.

Now, I am going to start by writing the introduction. We call the first paragraph of a report an introduction. It tells the reader in a few sentences what the report is going to be about. It's written in the present tense. The sentences need to be short and clear. We can use our note making wheel to help us plan our introduction. Let's look at your note wheels. What headings have you got? We can use these to plan what we put in the main part of our report. Let's see – one paragraph about things further from the school, another about things near the school and the third about the school itself. Now, our introduction needs to tell the reader quickly and clearly what the report will tell them. Let's see how we could start. I know – I will use those headings to write my first four sentences.'

This report is about the location of (name of your school) **School.** *I think I need to put a full stop there.* **It describes the area between the outskirts of the village/town/city and the school. It also describes the area immediately outside the school and the school grounds. Finally, it describes what the school itself is like.**

Ask the children to read them back with you.

Once you are sure the children understand how to go about writing an introduction, ask them to use their note making wheels to write their own introduction to the report. Remind them to keep it short and clear with only a few sentences.

Plenary

Share some of the children's introductions, commenting on them as you go. Ask them to share their writing with a response partner and to check that:

- the three main points are included;
- it is written in the present tense;
- the sentences start with capital letters and end with full stops;
- the information used is from the notes about the school.

Taking off

Learning objectives

■ To introduce the idea of paragraphs.

■ To organise notes into sentences.

■ To write the main body of a report.

Resources

■ The children's completed work from previous lessons

■ Large sheets of paper, strips of paper, felt-tipped pens

What to do

Explain to the children that they are going to use their notes to write the next part of the report on the location of their school.

Divide them into mixed ability groups. Tell them that each group is going to become an 'expert' on one part of the location of the school – 'the school', 'near the school' or 'further from the school'. Tell them that an expert is someone who knows and understands a lot about something and who can explain it clearly to others. Remind them of the audience for the final report – ideally you will have paired up with another local school.

Ask each group to read through their section of their notes and to talk about their section, asking and answering questions so that they feel at home with the information and are becoming 'expert'.

Demonstrate to the whole class how to use one section of their notes to write sentences. Display an enlarged copy of the completed note making wheel (Sheet D) from 'Switching on'. Read through 'the school' section with them. Ask them to pick out key points and phrases from their notes. You could ask: *'Which words and phrases are the most important in this section? That's right – small primary school. Where is it? (Lower Town Road) 'Let's highlight them.'* Go through the section with them, helping them to highlight key ideas.

Talk them through writing the first sentence. You could say, for example, *'We have highlighted "small" and "primary" and "Lower Town Road". Let's see how we could write that in the report. What about…* **It is a small primary school. It is on Lower Town Road.***? Do we need to add anything? Yes that's a good idea.* **It is a small primary school, located on Lower Town Road opposite some houses.**

Write the sentences on the board or flip chart and explain that in their groups they are going to use their own note making wheels to write some sentences in the same way. Tell them to highlight the key points first. Circulate among the children, helping them with their choices. Ask them to work together to write four sentences. These could be written on strips of paper in felt-tipped pen and then sticky-tacked onto a large sheet of sugar paper to display and share with the rest of the class. Circulate amongst the groups, emphasising choice of language and helping them to sort out the wording of each sentence. Read out good examples as you go.

Gather the class together again and ask each group to put their sheet up on display. Share the first group's work with the rest of the class. Point out the technical language and any linking words. You could say, *'Notice how they have used the word "facilities"; it is the correct "geography word" to use here.'* Talk about the order of the sentences. *'Does each sentence lead sensibly on to the next? Let's move one sentence strip and see which is the best order to put them in.'* Work out the best order for the sentences. Ask the group if they wish to change or add anything. Check the sentences together.

Ask the other groups to come up in turn, and this time ask the rest of the class for comments. You could say, *'What do you think of their sentences? Do they include all the points? Do they explain the points clearly? Have they chosen their words carefully? What sort of words have they used?'* and so on. You are looking for answers that include:

the sentences follow their notes;

they use geography words; (technical terms and subject specific language).

Ask the class if they think the sentences are in the right order. Discuss the order with them and agree on an order for the sentence strips. Repeat this activity with each group's work.

Explain to the children that each group's set of sentences work together to make a paragraph. Explain to them what a paragraph is. You could say, *'A paragraph is a group of sentences which give you information about a topic. The sentences link together to tell you more facts about the same thing. The facts in each paragraph of the report should refer back to the heading. If the heading is "The School" then the sentences must be about the school, not about things near the school or further from the school.'*

Ask the children to tell you which order the paragraphs should be in and move the sugar paper sheets to put the writing in the best order. Carry out a final check by reading all the paragraphs together.

Plenary

Put the children into their groups and ask them to pretend that one of them is a stranger to the area. Ask the others to tell them about the location of their school. Ask the groups to perform their role play. Ask the watchers to check that the information given is correct.

Before the next lesson, ask the children to complete the paragraphs for all three geographical areas by using the sentences from the other groups' work.

Writing across the Curriculum

Flying solo

Learning objective
- To write a conclusion to a report.

Resource
- Introduction and three paragraphs already written from previous lessons

What to do

Tell the children that they are going to complete their reports today by writing the conclusion. Ask them to remind you what a conclusion is. Agree that it sums up in a few sentences the main facts which the reader has learned from the report – it pulls the main ideas out of the report and reminds the reader what they have just read.

Put the children into mixed ability groups. Ask them to work in pairs within their groups. Tell them to read through their reports and decide which are the one or two most important points from each paragraph. They can highlight or underline them. Then ask each pair to compare and discuss their points with another pair in their group. Circulate amongst the groups, helping the children to clarify the idea of 'most important points'.

Do a shared writing session to model how to write a conclusion. Think aloud as you plan and write it. What you can say is in italics; what you write is in bold.

This will be the last paragraph of the report. The conclusion should be quite short and written in clear sentences. It tells the reader what the main points of the report are, quickly and simply. Let's look at the first paragraph. Most of you underlined 'small primary school', 'in a big village' and 'quiet street'. Now I need to put those ideas into a sentence. How could I write that in one or two sentences? Let's see. **This small primary school is situated in a quiet street in a big village.** *I need a full stop there. That tells us where it is and what sort of school. In the next paragraph you have underlined 'post office', 'church' and 'shops'. How can we write this as a sentence? Perhaps* **The village has a post office, shops and a church. They are all very near to the school.** *That tells us about the village facilities.*

Ask each group in turn to point out the main ideas of a paragraph and use their replies to write a sentence or two about each paragraph with them on the whiteboard/flip chart. Point out the technical vocabulary where it is used and talk about any linking words and phrases that you write. Remember to talk about the choice of language and the punctuation as you go.

Read the conclusion out to the class. Do they think it has summarised the report? You could ask: 'Do you think our conclusion has pulled out all the main points? Have we left anything out? Are the sentences in the right order? Have I remembered capital letters and full stops?' (Leave the odd one out to keep the children on their toes.)

Ask the children to look at the points they have picked out in their reports and ask them to use them to write four or five sentences to make their own conclusion.

Work with one group to extend their thinking and the quality of their writing. Talk to them about their choices of key points. Discuss any that seem less important which they may have included. Ask them to explain their choices. Demonstrate how to experiment with vocabulary, both to avoid repetition of the main text and also to improve descriptions. You could suggest an adjective or help them look up a synonym. Encourage the children in this group to think about the order of their sentences, which should mirror that of the main body of the report.

After they have completed their conclusions, ask them to work with a response partner to check their complete reports. Guide them through this by writing a checklist on the whiteboard. It should include the following:

- Read the report from beginning to end.
- Does the report have a title?
- Check each paragraph in turn.
- Do the sentences have capital letters and full stops that help the writing to make sense?

Writing Across the Curriculum   YEAR 3

- Is it written in the present tense?
- Is it written in the third person, no 'you', 'I' or 'we'?
- Does it use any special 'geography' words?
- Which is the best piece of writing in the report? Tell your partner why you like it!

Plenary

Ask the children to tell you what they have learned about their local area. Has writing the report helped them understand their area better? If they had to create a helpful hints sheet for another Year 3 class on how to write a good report, what things would they include? Agree a list.

The children could make a display of their information and invite another class to look at it. They could explain their display and reports to the visitors.

Sheet A

(title to say what the report is about)

Fir Tree Primary School

This is a report about Fir Tree Primary School. It describes where the school is located and what surrounds it. It also describes the places near the school and the facilities in the town.

(general nouns and pronouns)

(introduction to orientate the reader)

The location

Fir Tree Primary School is a small primary school, situated on the edge of town in Lower Town Road. It is by some fir trees, hence its name. It has a large playground. Opposite the school are some houses. Roads lead to other houses on the left as you look at the map. On the right the road leads to flats.

(non-chronological organisation)

(information organised in paragraphs)

Places near Fir Tree Primary School

Near the school are a supermarket and a computer factory. Next to the supermarket are a swimming pool and tennis courts. The tennis courts are near the golf course and the river. There are also a cafe, a library, a post office and some shops not far from the school. The shops and the library can be reached on foot by crossing
a pedestrian bridge.

(sub headings to organise paragraphs)

Facilities in the town

Further from the school are several blocks of flats that are opposite Fir Tree Comprehensive School. There is also another factory; this one makes car parts. There are a church and some more shops. Opposite the shops are a petrol station and the hospital. Over the bridge are an airport and a public house. This part of town is very busy.

(third person)

(present tense)

Fir Tree Primary School is on the quieter outskirts of the town. It is in a residential street with houses and flats. Shops, factories and sporting facilities are quite near the school. The town itself is big and busy.

(conclusion to sum up)

(technical words)

Writing Across the Curriculum

PHOTOCOPIABLE

Sheet B

Fir Tree Primary School

This is a report about Fir Tree Primary School. It describes where the school is located and what surrounds it. It also describes the places near the school and the facilities in the town.

The location

Fir Tree Primary School is a small primary school, situated on the edge of town in Lower Town Road. It is by some fir trees, hence its name. It has a large playground. Opposite the school are some houses. Roads lead to other houses on the left as you look at the map. On the right the road leads to flats.

Places near Fir Tree Primary School

Near the school are a supermarket and a computer factory. Next to the supermarket are a swimming pool and tennis courts. The tennis courts are near the golf course and the river. There are also a cafe, a library, a post office and some shops not far from the school. The shops and the library can be reached on foot by crossing a pedestrian bridge.

Facilities in the town

Further from the school are several blocks of flats that are opposite Fir Tree Comprehensive School. There is also another factory; this one makes car parts. There are a church and some more shops. Opposite the shops are a petrol station and the hospital. Over the bridge are an airport and a public house. This part of town is very busy.

Fir Tree Primary School is on the quieter outskirts of the town. It is in a residential street with houses and flats. Shops, factories and sporting facilities are quite near the school. The town itself is big and busy.

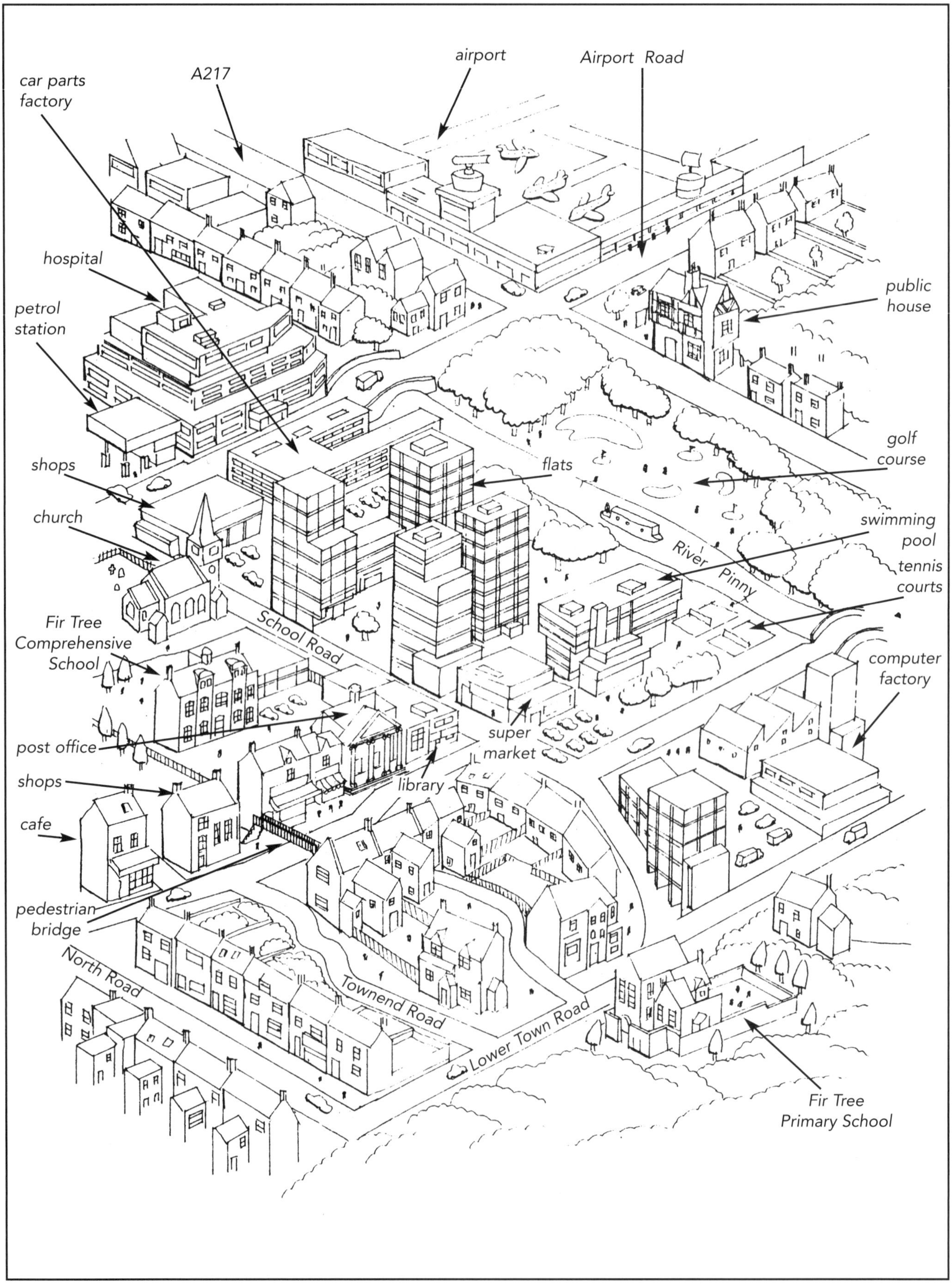
car parts factory
A217
airport
Airport Road
hospital
petrol station
public house
golf course
shops
flats
church
swimming pool
River Pinny
tennis courts
Fir Tree Comprehensive School
School Road
computer factory
post office
super market
shops
library
cafe
pedestrian bridge
North Road
Townend Road
Lower Town Road
Fir Tree Primary School

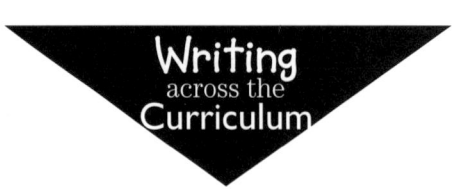

Sheet D

Note making wheel

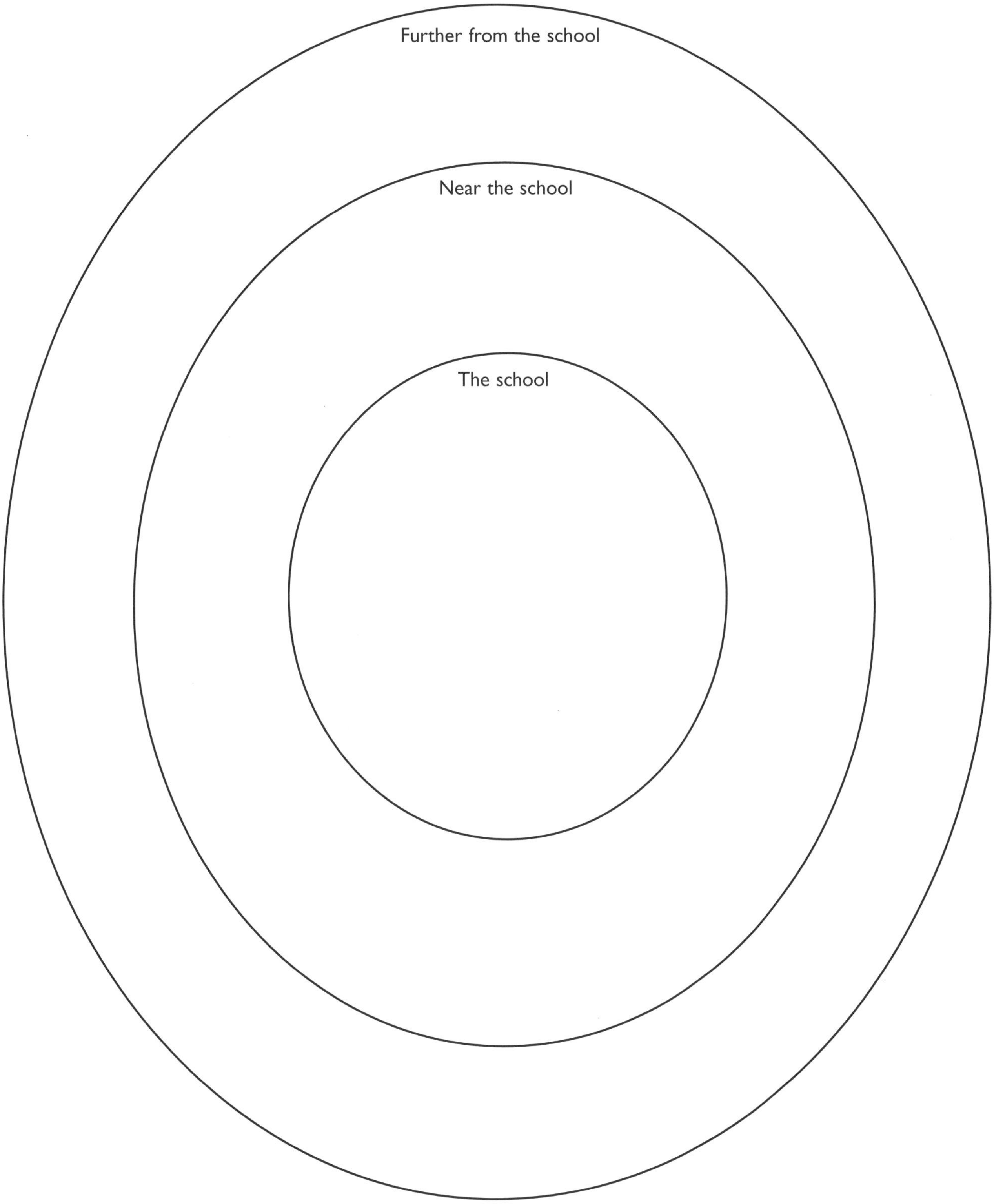

- Further from the school
- Near the school
- The school

Unit 2

Lesson focus
History Unit 8 – What were the differences between the lives of the rich and poor people in Tudor times?

Overall aim
To write a report that describes how the Tudor rich dressed, ate and worked.

History emphasis
This unit encourages children to find out about the way in which the rich and poor people lived in Tudor times by using a range of information sources.

Literacy links
Year 3, Term 1: T18, T20, T22, S11, S12

About this unit
In this unit, the children will develop their ability to find and use information for a specific purpose. They will use visual information (photos, artefacts), written information (non-fiction texts), spoken information (film, visitors) and ICT sources such as information CD-Roms.

Switching on

Learning objectives
- To identify the key words and phrases in a non-chronological report.
- To make notes.
- To use notes to write sentences.

Resources
- Sheet A (page 41)
- Pictures of poor people's housing in Tudor times

What to do
Tell the children they are going to learn about the differences between the rich and poor in Tudor times. Explain that over the next few lessons they are going to read some reports about poor Tudor people and then find out about rich Tudor people in order to write their own report later.

Ask them to tell you what they already know about the rich and poor in Tudor times. List their ideas.

Show the children an enlarged version of Sheet A and tell them that they are going to read the report in order to make some notes. Ask them to tell you what they think notes are. You want them to tell you they are key words and phrases chosen to help identify information you want to remember.

Read the report with the children and ask them to tell you what it is telling them. Show them more pictures of housing for the poor in Tudor times. Identify any features in the pictures that are mentioned in the report.

Ask them to find any special words in the report that help them to understand the main points in the paragraphs, such as 'peasant' and 'hearthstone'. Circle the words. List these words on the board or flip chart.

Read the report again (perhaps a child could read it) and ask the children to identify the main points. These could be underlined. Add these phrases to the list of words. Explain that the list of words and phrases represents some notes about the report.

Tell them that you are now going to show them how they can use the notes to write their own sentences about houses for the poor in Tudor times.

Following is a script you can use or adapt. Remember to think out loud, adding and revising as you go to help them understand the writing process. What you say is in italics; what you write is in bold.

Writing across the Curriculum

First of all we will need to give the first paragraph a subheading – we can use the same one as in the text: **Introduction**.

Now, let's look at some of the first notes we made from the introduction: poor people/called peasants/lived simple lives/ small amount of money/inexpensive materials. Let's think about how we could turn these notes into sentences. We need to say who it is about and what it is about and when it was…

I know – let's start by writing **Poor people were called peasants. They had little money. Their houses were simple and built from cheap materials.** *Let's read it through together. Could we add anything? Do we need to change anything? That's a good point – we need to say when it was, so let's add* **in Tudor times** *to the end of our first sentence. Now let's read it right through again.*

Poor people were called peasants in Tudor times. They had little money. Their houses were simple and built from cheap materials.

Now we'll look at our notes for the second paragraph about the houses. First, let's put the heading: **The Houses of the Poor.** *Now, which do you think are the most important points we have put in our notes? That's right, they were huts. Yes, we do need to say what they were made from. So let's draft our first sentence.* **They lived in huts made from cob. This was a mixture of straw, mud and lime.** *What about the roof? That's right, we could put* **They had thatched roofs.** *What about the size of the huts? Let's look back at our notes. What do we need to add?* **The huts were small with only one or two rooms.**

Continue in this way, writing the main points of the second paragraph with the children. Read it through together.

Ask the children to write their own sentences about the poor, using the notes on the flip chart. They could work in pairs to support each other. Remind them that they can use subheadings – the same as in the text or some of their own. The third paragraph is about inside the houses, the last paragraph is the conclusion. While the children are doing this, read their work and read out and praise good examples.

Plenary

Ask the children to read their sentences to each other in pairs and check that they have used all the information from the flip chart.

Ask them what they have learned about the poor in Tudor times? Start a Tudor word bank.

Revving up

Learning objectives

- To identify the key features of a non-chronological report.
- To learn how notes can be expanded to write sentences.

Resources

- Sheets B and C (pages 42 and 43)
- Word bank from previous lesson
- Pictures of Tudor poor showing clothing, food and lifestyle

What to do

Ask the children to tell you what they remember about the houses of the poor in Tudor times. Ask them to tell you how they got their information. (You want them to remember about reading a report and making notes.)

Explain that they are now going to share some more notes about the poor in Tudor times in order to learn how the notes could be written up as a report.

Share an enlarged version of Sheet B. Identify new words and discuss what they mean (such as 'comfits' = sweets). Add these words to the word bank from the previous lesson.

Ask the children to work in pairs for a few minutes to read through the notes again and talk about the information in them. Put key questions on the board to help them interpret the notes; for example:

- What did the poor eat most of the time?
- Which food was not often eaten by the poor?
- What did people eat on Fridays?

YEAR 3   Writing Across the Curriculum

- What did poor people drink?
- What materials were poor people's clothes made from?
- What did women wear?
- What did men wear?
- Where did most poor people live?
- What work did they do?
- What did poor people do for fun?

Share what they found out. Show them the pictures of the Tudor poor. Can they identify anything in the pictures that is mentioned in the notes?

Show an enlarged version of Sheet C with the annotations covered up. Explain that it is a report that has been written using the notes they have just read. Tell them that a report is written and set out in a special way, making it different from other types of writing. Without reading the report, ask them to tell you what they immediately notice about it. (Title, subheadings, paragraphs and so on.)

Read the report, sharing the structural and linguistic features by uncovering each annotation one at a time. Make sure the children understand the meanings of the terms.

Show them how the notes (from Sheet B) have been made into the report by explaining how the words have been written up into sentences. You could do this by underlining words in the notes that are contained in the report and sharing ideas about how a sentence could be formed from them.

Tell the children that in the next few lessons they are going to make their own notes and use them to write sentences for their own report.

Plenary

Ask the children to tell you what they have learned about writing a report. You are looking for the points made in the annotations on Sheet C – title, introduction, subheadings, paragraphs, impersonal voice, past tense, some technical language and a brief conclusion. Write their responses on a flip chart to use as a 'memory jogger' for the next session.

Taking off

Learning objectives

- To revise the features of a non-chronological report.
- To make notes.
- To use notes to write sentences.
- To plan a report.

Resources

- Sheets D and E (pages 44 and 45)
- Posters, pictures and books about the life of the Tudor rich

What to do

Tell the children that today they are going to investigate how the rich lived in Tudor times. Share the posters and pictures in the books about the Tudor rich with them. Ask them to tell you how they think the rich lived and what they did. Note their ideas on the board or flip chart.

Show an enlarged version of Sheet D and explain that it contains some notes about rich people in Tudor times. Discuss the meaning of the words in bold and add them to the notes on the board.

Remind the children that notes use key words to remind the writer of the important information they need to remember. Explain that you want them to find out some more about the rich in Tudor times and add some notes of their own to the sheet.

Divide the children into pairs and provide them with a copy of Sheet D and some reference sources. Ask them each to find as much information as they can about one aspect of being rich; for example, 'What clothes did the rich wear?'

After about 15 minutes, ask one child from each pair to sit with a different partner who has been researching a different aspect of being rich in Tudor times. Ask them to tell each other what they found out and to make notes on their sheet. Do this again until all three areas on the note making sheet are completed.

Tell them they are now going to plan a report on how the rich lived in Tudor times. Recap what a report is and how it is set out. Show them an enlarged version of Sheet E and explain that this will help them to plan their report. Ask them to write three (or more) sentences for each section, using their own and the original notes. Walk around the class as they are doing this and read out good sentences to the rest.

Plenary

Ask the children what they have learned about the rich in Tudor times.

Ask some of the children to read out their planning work. Share ideas about sentence construction and check they have used capital letters and full stops correctly.

Flying solo

Learning objective

- To write a report.

Resources

- Sheet C (page 43)
- The children's work from previous lesson

What to do

Tell the children that they are now going to write their report about the Tudor rich, using their report planning sheet (Sheet E). Show an enlarged version of Sheet C to remind them about the structural and linguistic features of a report text.

Explain that to help them get started on their own report you are going to show them how to write the introduction.

Decide with them on a title for the report; remind them that it tells the reader what the report is about. Write it on the flip chart/whiteboard. Ask them to remind you what an introduction does. You are looking for replies that explain that it is made up of a few short sentences that let the reader know what the report is about. Talk the children through the questions in the introduction box of the planning frame. Explain that answering the 'who?', 'what?' and 'when?' questions will help them to write the introduction.

Below is a script you can use or adapt. What you say is in italics; what you write is in bold.

Let's start by saying who our report is about. **This report is about rich people.** *Now let's answer the question 'When?' We can add 'in Tudor times', so our first sentence now reads* **This report is about rich people in Tudor times.** *Then we can add what it is about.* **It tells us how rich people lived.** *I think we could add another sentence to explain just a little bit more.* **Many of them lived in or near London to be near the king.** *Did they have a special name? Yes, that's right. We could add* **They were called nobles.**

Let's read the whole introduction together.

This report is about rich people in Tudor times. It tells us how rich people lived. Many of them lived in or near London to be near the king. They were called nobles.

Then ask the children to use each section of the planning frame to write their own reports.

While they are working, choose a group to work alongside. You could work with a less able group, helping them to decide on three main points for the introduction and talking them through the composition of their sentences. Able children should be encouraged to add a little more information to their introduction – perhaps including some technical language but it should be no more than four or five short clear sentences.

After about 20 minutes, ask the children to find a partner to read their report to. Does their report make sense? Have they used a title and headings in their report? Have they used capital letters and full stops? Have they used special history words? Ask the children to suggest any improvements that could be made. Have they written a short conclusion summing up the main points of the report?

Plenary

Ask the children to tell you which people, the poor or the rich, they think had the better lives and why. Ask them what are the important things they have learned in order to write a report. Using their answers, write a brief 'Report writing guide' that can be displayed as a literacy resource for them to refer to in the future.

Sheet A

Houses of the Tudor poor

Introduction

*In Tudor times poor people were called **peasants**. They lived simple lives and often worked on the land. They only earned a small amount of money. Their homes were basic; they were small and simply built from inexpensive materials.*

The houses of the poor

*Poor people lived in **huts**. These were made from **cob**. Cob was made up of a mixture of mud, lime and straw. The finished walls were often painted white, pink or yellow. The **loft** was covered by a **thatched** roof. The thatch was made from dried reeds or straw. The huts were small and had only one or two rooms. The family would often sleep together, all in one room. The huts had small openings for windows. These were covered by wooden shutters or sacking flaps to keep out the draughts. They could not afford to use glass, which was very expensive. The doors were fastened by a simple latch made from wood. The floor was made from **hardened** earth.*

Inside the houses of the poor

*The fire was on a **hearthstone** which had a hood made from **basketwork** sealed with clay to help take the smoke out of the **smoke hole**. There was very little furniture. They would sit on simple **stools**. They cooked with only a few pots. They had a large wooden box or **chest** to store things in.*

Conclusion

In Tudor times, poor people lived in huts made from local materials. The huts were small and simply made. They did not have glass in their windows. They had no money for decorations or luxuries.

Sheet B

Notes on the Tudor poor

Clothing: cheap
made from wool or fustian (coarse cotton)

Men: breeches, jerkins (sleeveless leather jackets), leggings, leather shoes

Women: dresses with quite short skirts, aprons, cloth stockings, white woollen caps, leather shoes

Food: Usually –
bread
soup made from vegetables

Not often –
meat – beef, mutton, bacon, chicken, goose, duck and game
(meat was salted to preserve it)

people had to eat fish on Fridays
comfits were popular if they could buy them

Drink: ale, cider and wine poured from leather jugs into mugs of horn

Lifestyle: Most people lived in the country. They:
kept animals
grew wheat and barley crops
sold what was left in the towns

Some worked:
on looms, spinning
in mines
on ships, fishing

For fun they:
went to plays, watched bull baiting and cock fighting, danced and sang on feast days

Sheet C

Writing across the Curriculum

The poor in Tudor times

(title to say what the report is about)

(introduction to orientate the reader)

This report is about how the poor lived in Tudor times. The poor had difficult lives and some were beggars. Most lived in the countryside and were called peasants.

What the poor wore

(sub-headings to organise paragraphs)

Poor people wore clothes made out of wool or fustian. Men wore breeches that reached to their knees. They also wore jerkins made from leather and woollen leggings. They wore leather shoes. Women wore dresses with skirts below their knees and aprons. They wore white woollen caps on their heads. They also wore leather shoes.

(information organised in paragraphs)

What the poor ate

(past tense (historical report))

Poor people did not have a lot of food to eat. They usually ate bread. They would also have soup made from vegetables. When they could they would eat meat such as beef, mutton, bacon or game. In winter the meat was salted to preserve it. People ate fish on Fridays if they had any. Comfits were popular if they could afford them. They drank beer, cider or wine, as water was not always safe to drink.

(third person)

How the poor lived

Most poor people lived in the country. They kept animals and grew wheat and barley. They sold what they had left in the towns. Some might have worked on looms, spinning, or in the mines to earn money. People went to sea to fish. For fun they went to plays and danced and sang on feast days. They might watch bull baiting or cock fighting.

The poor in Tudor times worked hard to live. They mostly lived in the country where they worked to get food to eat. On feast days they enjoyed themselves dancing and singing. Poor people had hard lives in Tudor times.

(technical words)

(conclusion to sum up)

(non-chronological organisation)

PHOTOCOPIABLE

Writing Across the Curriculum

Sheet D

Writing across the Curriculum

Notes on the Tudor rich

	My own notes

Clothing:
 Men:
    silk shirts, padded **doublets** with slits, short breeches, velvet stockings, flat hats with feathers
 Women:
    embroidered dresses of velvet, **bodices**, skirts, **farthingales** with stiffened hoops, big sleeves, damask **petticoats**, hats with jewels sewn in them
 Both men and women: velvet cloaks, fur-lined cloaks
 	
 Food: Large meals of rich food
    Breakfast:
       beer and bread
    Dinner:
       meat, vegetables and beer, cider or wine
    Supper:
       often a **banquet** in the large homes of the very rich
       beef, mutton, pork, game, **poultry** and fish
       cabbage and onions, fruit and nuts
       cakes, jellies and **comfits**
 	
 Lifestyle:
    owned land – their peasants farmed it for them
    built gardens
    were **merchants** who traded
    spent time at **court**
    went to theatres
    played cards and dice
    hunted if they were **nobles**
    went to bear gardenss
    enjoyed celebrating feast days
    danced
	Clothing:
	
	 Food:
	
	 Lifestyle:

Writing Across the Curriculum

PHOTOCOPIABLE

Sheet E

Title: _____

Introduction
Write a few sentences to help the reader understand what the report is going to be about. They should answer the questions: 'Who is it about?', 'What is it about?' and 'When is it about?'

Clothing
Write a few sentences about the clothes the Tudor rich wore.

The clothes the rich people wore were…

Food
Write a few sentences about the food rich people ate.

Rich people ate very well. They enjoyed eating…

Lifestyle
Write a few sentences about what rich people did in Tudor times.

In Tudor times rich people did different things, such as…

Conclusion
Write a few sentences to sum up the main points of the report.

Writing across the Curriculum

Chapter 3

Instruction writing

What is an instruction text?

Instructions tell someone how to do or make something. The success of the instructions can be judged by how easily the reader (or listener) can follow the procedure successfully.

Structural features

- Heading and subheadings
- List of items required
- Sequence of steps to be carried out in order
- Often has labelled diagrams

Linguistic features

- Usually written in the imperative mood
- Sentences begin with an imperative verb, 'you' or a time connective such as 'then', 'next', 'after that'
- Clear and concise – no unnecessary adjectives, adverbs or 'flowery' language

Examples of instruction texts

- recipes
- directions
- instructions for games
- technical manuals
- sewing or knitting patterns

Teaching instruction writing

One of the fundamental challenges of teaching children to write instructions is to help them consider purpose, audience and form. It is essential that they consider the prior knowledge and needs of their intended readers in order to write effective instructions that the readers can follow. Stress the importance of thinking yourself into the mind of the reader and anticipating their needs. As in writing poetry, children need to exercise some discipline in choosing just the right words and exercising economy of words so their sentences are generally simple with clear sequencing and precise language that can be easily understood by the reader. It is good to have readers using the instructions to test out the extent of the success of the writing.

While it is generally taught that instructions begin with an imperative verb, they can also begin with the word 'you' or a time connective. Children should be given freedom to judge which sort of sentence beginning is most appropriate. There is a good opportunity here to discuss the differences between the two different forms of instructional communication – speaking and listening and writing and reading – and the demands they make upon children.

Instruction writing - progression

Simple instructions are introduced in Key Stage 1. (Reception: T15; Year 1, Term 1: T13, T16; Year 2, Term 1: T13, T14, T15, T16, T17, T18)

In **Year 3** children evaluate different types of instructional texts and are introduced to a range of organisational devices when writing instructions such as lists, bullet points and keys (Term 2: T12, T13, T14, T15, T16).

In Year 4 the key features of instructional texts are taught (Term: 1 T22) and children learn to write instructions using linking phrases and organisational devices, such as subheadings and numbers (Term 1: T25, T26).

In Year 5 (Term 1: T22, T25) and Year 6 (Term 3: T19, T22) children are moving onto writing and testing instructions, by revising the structure, organisational and presentational devices and language features of their instructions.

Writing across the Curriculum

Unit 1

Lesson focus
Music Unit 10 – Play it again – exploring rhythmic patterns using tuned and untuned instruments

Overall aim
To write instructions that explain clearly how to perform an extended composition using instruments they have made for the purpose.

Music emphasis
This unit encourages the children to explore sounds and rhythmic patterns. They create sequences and combinations of sounds. They compose and perform music using a variety of rhythmic instruments, some of which they have made themselves.

Literacy links
Year 3, Term 2: T12, T13, T16

About this unit
This unit introduces the children to the idea of simple rhythmic patterns, in particular ostinato. They will create their own patterns and give instructions to others on how to play them. They will make some simple musical instruments and write instructions on how to make them. They will explore different timbres and dynamics to make their music interesting to listen to.

The tasks reinforce and extend the children's understanding of rhythm and develop cooperation and teamwork skills through paired and group work. The children will develop their ability to read and follow instructions and to make and sequence correctly instructions of their own. They will write text and notation that instruct other children how to play the rhythms themselves.

Switching on

Learning objectives
- To understand the features of an instruction text.
- To follow instructions to make a musical instrument.
- To play different rhythms on a musical instrument.
- To understand the term 'rhythm'

Resources
- Sheet A (page 53)
- Materials to make the rhythm board – as listed on Sheet A (enough for one board per pair of children)
- A word bank made up of the following words: duration, rhythm, tempo, steady, fast, slow, beats, sequence, notation, half, quarter, compose, performance, instruments.

What to do
Show the children the word bank. Tell them that they are going to make some musical instruments and that they will need to know the meaning of some musical terms.

Discuss the meanings of the words with them. Also explain the following terms, giving examples: ostinato – a repeated rhythm, such as four slow beats clapped or tapped out and repeated throughout a sequence; rhythmic pattern (texture) – combined rhythmic patterns, such as a slow single beat combined with four steady beats.

Tell the children they are going to make a rhythm board, following some instructions you will give them. (Have all the equipment you need already prepared.) Explain that they will also practise playing different rhythms on the rhythm board. Ask them to remind you what 'rhythm' means and to suggest what they think a rhythm board might be.

Tap out a few different rhythms and ask them to listen carefully and repeat them back to you. You can sit them in a circle and tap out a short repeated rhythm using clapping. Try two short and two long beats as an introductory sequence. Ask the children to repeat the rhythm as a group and then tap out a rhythm for one

YEAR 3 Writing Across the Curriculum 47

child to copy, and the next to copy, until the rhythm has been passed round the circle.

Now tell them that you are going to give them the instructions to make the rhythm board. Say that you are going to read out the instructions and that they have to listen very carefully in order to know how to make their rhythm boards. Read out the instructions from Sheet A.

Ask the children to repeat the instructions to you. Write the instructions they remember on the board. Ask them to tell you if they think they have remembered everything. Do the instructions make sense? Are they in the right sequence?

Share an enlarged version of Sheet A and compare their version with the instructions on the sheet. Did they remember everything? Point out the importance of the instructions being in a particular order. Discuss how useful it is to have written instructions rather than verbal ones and how diagrams can help us to understand what the sentences mean.

Put the children into pairs. Tell them that they will now use the instructions to make their rhythm boards. Ask one of the pair to collect the items they need as you read them out and to take them to their table. When this is done, read out each instruction, one at a time, demonstrate it and then ask the children to carry it out themselves.

When the rhythm boards are made, tap out a rhythm on your board and ask the children to repeat it on their boards. Ask them to count out the beats to the next rhythm you tap out and repeat it back to you. Next, ask one of each pair to clap a rhythm and the other to play it. Vary the rhythms but do not make them too long – keep to a steady, rhythmic beat.

Set a short task – ask the children to make a clapping and tapping rhythm, which can be repeated three times. Ask them to demonstrate their rhythms to the others.

Plenary

Ask the children to tell you what they have learned about following instructions, oral and written. Share an enlarged version of Sheet A again and point out the particular features of instruction texts, such as:

- heading and subheadings;
- a list of items required;
- a sequence of steps to be carried out;
- labelled diagrams;
- written in the imperative;

  short, clear sentences.

Revving up

Learning objectives

■ To understand the importance of sequencing in instructions.

■ To put instructions in order.

■ To follow instructions.

■ To recognise that different rhythmic instruments can produce different sounds.

■ To use different sounds to create a rhythmic pattern.

Resources

■ Sheet B (page 54) – two copies: one to enlarge and one to cut up

■ A collection of empty containers, such as washing-up liquid bottles, plastic milk bottles and small plastic containers (all with their lids)

■ Objects that can be used to make rhythmic sounds, such as very small pebbles, rice, lentils, dried peas, buttons, washed sand, water

■ Rhythm boards and thimbles (or other objects that can be used to tap out a sound) from previous lesson

What to do

Ask the children if they can tell you what instructions are for and what the special features of instruction texts are. You want them to remember that they tell you how to do something; they have a title and subheadings; they are written in simple sentences in order and that the steps can be numbered.

Tell the children that they are going to make another musical instrument today, using some different instructions. Share an enlarged version of Sheet B. Ask them to tell you if the instructions make sense. What do they need to do in order to follow the instructions?

Ask them to scan the page and find the title for the instructions. When they have, use your cut up version of Sheet B to sticky-tack this to a board. Ask them to tell you which part of the instructions they think should go next. Agree this and place this piece under the title. Repeat this process until the class is happy that all the instructions are in the correct order. Number the instructions.

Tell the children to work in the same pairs as in the previous lesson to follow the instructions to make the new instrument. Arrange the containers and objects in groups on a table so that they can take it in turns to come and choose a balanced selection of objects to make their sounds. You might prefer to ask each pair to use different resources from others so that there is a variety of instruments available for playing at the end of the session.

When the instructions have been followed and the instruments made, ask the children to sit in fours. They should pair up with another pair that have different rhythmic instruments.

Ask the children to use their rhythm bsoard and their new instruments to make the same rhythms as in the previous lesson, using different sounds. Remind them about the rhythmic patterns they developed and explain that you now want them to select one of the rhythms and develop it – but to keep it simple. Explain that they need to think about using the instruments at different times in the rhythm as well as all together.

Give them time to develop their rhythms and then ask them to play them to the rest of the class.

Demonstrate ways of recording their rhythm patterns. If your children are used to using invented notation such as dash, dash, dot, dot you could continue with this.

You could introduce musical notation – a semibreve (𝆒), which is equal to four crotchets; a minim (𝅗𝅥) – equal to two crotchets – and a crotchet (𝅘𝅥). Four crotchets equal one semibreve.

Ask a confident pair to write their rhythm on the board. Ask the other children to play it. Repeat the activity two or three times until the children have understood how to write the notation you are using.

Ask the children to write their notation out on a long strip of paper so that the rhythm can be seen as a whole. Put the notations up around the room and ask the children to play the different rhythm patterns. (Earplugs may be useful at this point!) For example:

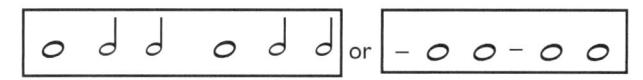

| o 𝅗𝅥 𝅗𝅥 o 𝅗𝅥 𝅗𝅥 | or | – o o – o o |

Plenary

Ask the children what they have learned about instructions today. They should be able to identify the importance of correct sequencing and know that instructions can be written in different ways.

Ask them to give you feedback about swapping their rhythmic recordings. Could others follow them easily?

What were the problems, if any?

Between now and the next lesson, ask the children to bring in a piece of music they enjoy that has good rhythms. It may be a piece they can play themselves. Say that you will also bring in a piece for them to listen to. Then play their choices and ask them to explain why they chose them. Can they beat out the rhythm? What does it make them feel?

Play your choice at the end – maybe Beethoven's fifth symphony or a similar rhythmic piece – and ask the children to clap, sing or chant the rhythm.

Writing across the Curriculum

Taking off

Learning objectives

- To develop rules for writing instructions.
- To draft a set of instructions.
- To use language to describe sounds and rhythms.
- To develop a performance using different sounds and rhythms.

Resources

- Sheet C (page 55)
- A selection of percussion instruments, such as triangles, drums, tambourines, tubular bells, xylophones, castanets, bongos and steel drums
- The rhythm board and sound instruments previously made by the children

What to do

Tell the children that today they are going to plan and develop a set of instructions for a performance of a rhythmic piece of music they have composed.

Ask them to tell you what they remember about the rhythms they have used and listened to in previous lessons. What was interesting about them? Why did they like some and not others?

Ask them to tell you what they remember about clapping and beating out simple rhythms on their instruments. Revisit the work covered on using rhythms to make different effects.

Introduce the idea of using rhythmic sounds to create a mood. Ask the children to tell you what sorts of moods music makes them feel. Write their responses on the board.

Discuss the sorts of words they could use to describe music that shows the listener different moods. You could use the categories of happy, sad, angry, lonely or frightening, for example. Ask them to tell you whether fast and slow rhythms can change the mood. Is a fast rhythm exciting and a slow rhythm soothing?

Put the children into groups of four to six and ask them to make up a rhythm. Tell them to decide on the following things. You could list them on the board.

- Decide if the music will be happy, sad, lonely, angry or frightening and whether it should be played slowly, quickly or at a medium pace.
- Decide which instruments you are going to use. You must use the rhythm boards, two of the instruments your group has made and two percussion instruments.
- Make up a rhythm that suits the mood you have decided on.
- Play the rhythm on the instruments you have chosen. Decide what order the instruments should be played in. Which instruments will you play together? Which instruments will be silent at times?
- When you are happy that you have the right sound and rhythm, write down the patterns of sound that each group member has used three times so that you repeat the pattern. Do this in the same way as in 'Revving up', using long strips of paper. Draw a picture at the beginning of the strip to show which instrument you have used. (See below.)

picture of instrument	notation

picture of instrument	notation

Once each group has completed their notation strips, ask them to follow them to play them again, in order to check that they have the right sequence and order for their composition.

Ask each group to perform their composition. Can the others identify what mood it is representing? Is it fast, slow or medium paced?

Ask the children how they could give instructions to another group so that they could play the piece themselves. Ask them to recall all the features that good

50 Writing Across the Curriculum   YEAR 3

instructions should have. Write a checklist on the board that includes:

- a title and subheadings;
- a list of things needed;
- an order in which to carry out the instructions;
- simple sentences (or symbols);
- a direct voice – 'you' to carry out the task.

Ask them to tell you what else they need to think about so that another group could play their composition successfully.

Show the children an enlarged version of Sheet C. Explain that they can use this to plan their instructions. Read the sheet through with them and model writing a set of instructions. Ask for a title and write it in. Talk about the first subheading and ask them to decide which items they would need to list for their piece of music. Write in a list from one of the groups. Do the same for the second section of the sheet. Remind the children about putting the instructions in the correct order. Ask them if it would be helpful to number the instructions.

Ask the children to work in pairs and provide them with their own copy of Sheet C to draft their own instructions. Walk around the classroom while the children are working, reading out good examples of instructions. Collect the instructions in and have them to give out in the 'Flying solo' lesson.

Plenary

Ask the children to give each other verbal instructions on playing their instrument(s). They should think about the sort of things they will say to each other. How will they give instructions? Will they tell the person that they should pick up the instrument, how they should hold it and how to play it? Give them time to think about this.

Ask a confident pair to demonstrate how they would give instructions to each other to play the instrument. Write the instructions on the board. Ask the others if they could follow the instructions and play the instrument. (You want them to tell you whether the instructions are clear, in the right order and use the direct voice – 'you'. You want them to realise that verbal instructions can include demonstration but written instructions may not.)

Tell the children that in the next lesson they are going to write a final set of instructions using their draft instructions on how to play their rhythm composition.

Flying solo

Learning objectives

- To write instructions.
- To follow instructions.

Resources

- Instruction plans from previous lesson
- Instruments from previous lesson

What to do

Revisit the work done on rhythm with the class. Ask the children to listen carefully and clap a rhythm back to you. Tell them to collect their instruments and sit in a circle. Ask different children to tap out or shake a rhythm and ask the others to copy it. Remind them that they are listening to audible instructions when they do this. Ask them what other sorts of instructions there are. (You want them to tell you about written instructions and the notation they have been using.)

Tell the children that today you want them to use their instruction plans from the previous lesson to write their final set of instructions. Tell them first to get into their playing groups and play the rhythm again to make sure their notation strips are correct and that they are happy with their composition and instruction plans.

Then ask them to work in pairs to write their instructions. After a little while, ask each pair to swap instructions with another pair in their group to see if they can follow the instructions easily. Ask the pairs to help each other improve the instructions for their group.

While the children are working in their groups, check to see that they are coping with the task. You may need to work with some pairs to help them organise their instructions and present them to another group. You should be checking that they have a title and are using the subheadings of 'What you need' and 'What to do'. Refer to their planning sheets (Sheet C). Have they followed them carefully and given enough instructions to make it easy for the group reading them to carry them out? When the children have completed their instructions, ask them to swap them with another group to see if they can follow them to successfully play the music.

When the children have read and followed the instructions, give them time to practise the composition and ask the different groups to play the piece, using the instructions they have been following. Ask the original group to play the piece. Do they sound the same?

Plenary

Discuss with the children how following the instructions worked. Were there problems? What were they? How could they be sorted out? What have they learned about writing instructions that people have to follow? (You want them to tell you that a title, subheadings and a sensible order of instructions are needed. The written instructions should be easy to understand and carry out.)

Ask a group who thought the instructions that they were given were clear and easy to follow to play the composition. Ask the children who wrote the instructions if they think that they were followed correctly.

Put up the instructions for playing and allow the children to look at them and try playing those they have not already tried. This will give the children confidence in reading and following instructions and reinforce the writing that they have done in this lesson in an auditory and visual way.

At the end of the session play some rhythmic music and ask the children to listen to it carefully and pick out a rhythm they like and to repeat it on their instrument. You could ask individual children to do this as a way of ending the instruction writing lesson with some rhythmic music that they can enjoy listening to and copying.

Sheet A

How to make and play a rhythm board

What you need

- ❑ a piece of hardboard or thick cardboard 25cm long x 15cm wide (Figure 1)
- ❑ two strips of foil or coloured card 15cm long x 4cm wide
- ❑ five plastic or metal thimbles or other objects that can be used to make a sound when tapped, such as spoons, short pieces of dowel or pencils
- ❑ scissors
- ❑ sticking tape

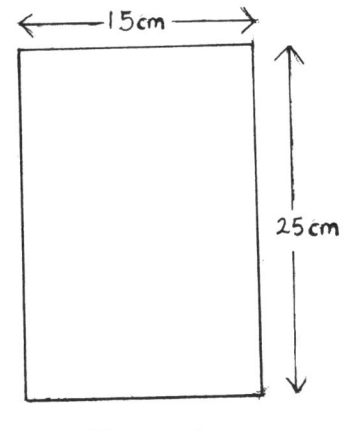

Figure 1

What to do

1. Take a piece of the coloured card or foil and fold it in half so that each side is about 2cm wide.

2. Place the foil or card over one end of the board (Figure 2).

3. Attach the foil or card in place using sticking tape.

4. Repeat instructions 1, 2 and 3 so that the other end of the board is covered with a piece of foil or card too.

5. Decorate your rhythm board to make it easy to recognise as the one you and your partner will use.

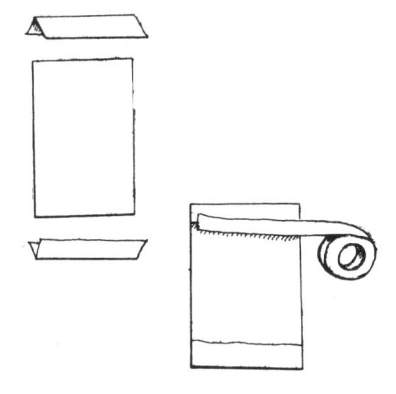

Figure 2

How to play the rhythm board

1. Place the thimbles on the fingers of one hand or hold a tapping object such as a spoon or pencil.

2. Hold one end of the board with the other hand and rest the other end on your knee or a table.

3. Tap out a rhythm on the board, using the thimbles or other tapping object.

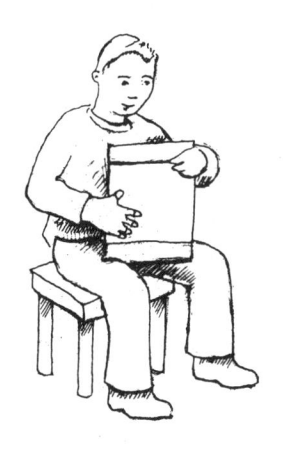

Sheet B

Writing across the Curriculum

Put a quarter of the objects into the container and put the lid on.

How to make a rhythmic instrument

Undo the lid and add another quarter of the objects to the container. Put the lid back on tightly.

What to do:

With a quarter of the objects inside, try a short rhythm test by shaking, rattling and rolling the container. Think about which sound you like best.

Firstly, check that the container is clean and the lid fits properly.

Decide which sound you like best – try a quarter, two quarters or all of the objects inside the container. If you need to empty out any objects, undo the lid, empty them out and then put the lid back on tightly.

Write on the container whether it is a shake, rattle or roll instrument.

What you need:
- a plastic container with a tight-fitting lid
- objects that you think will make an interesting sound
- a felt-tipped pen

Finally, undo the lid once more and add the rest of the objects. Put the lid back on. Repeat the rhythm test.

Repeat the rhythm test with two quarters of the objects inside the container.

Sheet C

Writing across the Curriculum

Write your title here.

How to _____

What you need

List the things the group will need in order to play your composition. Use your notation strips.

What to do

Think about the things the group needs to do:
- Do they need to collect the instruments?
- Do they need to read the notation strips?
- Do they need to practise the composition?
- When do they need to perform it?
- Can they ask for help from the group who made the piece up?

List your instructions and number them carefully.

PHOTOCOPIABLE

Unit 2

Lesson focus
Design and Technology Unit 3D – Photograph frames

Literacy links
Year 3, Term 2: T16

Overall aim
To write instructions that explain clearly how to make a freestanding photograph frame.

Design and Technology emphasis
This unit encourages the children to explore ways of making paper and card strong. They will learn why it is necessary for structures to be stable and will show evidence of this learning by making a strong and stable photo frame. They will select and use appropriate joining techniques and will be encouraged to talk about their work.

About this unit
In this unit the children will use practical D&T activities as a starting point to make simple annotated diagrams, sequenced notes and lists. They will follow simple instructions to carry out a simple task and also put model instructions in the correct order. They will develop their ability to write and sequence simple instructions before finally using the same practical activity, annotated diagram, and sequenced lists format to write a full set of instructions for making a free standing photograph frame. The children will learn how to strengthen paper and card in a variety of ways and how to select and use appropriate joining techniques. They will use what they have learned to design and make a freestanding photograph frame.

Switching on

Learning objectives
- To draw a simple annotated diagram.
- To follow instructions.

Resources
- Paper, card, scissors, different types of fastenings, such as glues, tapes, paperclips
- Some ready-made examples of how to strengthen or fasten card/paper, such as several thicknesses of card glued together and paper folded and clipped together

What to do
Tell the children that during the next few lessons they will find out about different types of picture and photograph frames in order to make their own. Explain that first they are going to explore different ways of making paper and card stronger and different ways of joining paper and card in order to help them make a good final picture frame themselves.

Ask the children to tell you ways they already know for making card and paper stronger (such as folding, rolling, layering and so on). Record their ideas on the board. Discuss what stiffened card could be used for (for example, making bridges that will take a load, a roof on a model or a stand for a picture).

Briefly demonstrate some of their simpler ideas using the card and paper. Show them the examples you made earlier of some of the more complicated methods, such as several layers of card glued together or concertinaed paper inside a paper tube.

Then ask them to give you ideas for joining paper and card, such as using sticking tapes, glues, paperclips and so on. Add these ideas to the list on the board. You could ask questions to prompt their thinking, such as *'How did you fix legs/doors on your last model?', 'Was it easy to do?', 'Was it strong enough for the job?'* and *'How can you use the paperclips to make a stronger join with glue?'*

Divide the children into pairs and provide them with paper, card and joining materials, such as different types of glue, tapes and fasteners. Ask them to spend time experimenting with different ways to make paper and card stronger as well as different ways of joining them together. Encourage them to talk to each other about what they are doing, and why.

After the children have had time to experiment, ask them to choose one of their ideas (of strengthening or fastening). Explain that you want them to make simple annotated diagrams so that other people could learn how to use their method. Tell them that first you will show them how to do this. You might like to prepare a suitable word bank, prior to the lesson, of words the children might use and put this on display.

Select one of the children's methods. Ask them to talk you through the techniques they have used to strengthen or fasten their paper/card, step by step. Then ask the others how they think they might begin writing this method down. Begin with the title. Ask them to choose a title, of the 'How to …' variety. Write this on the board. Then draw and label pictures to show each step. Try to keep to a small number of stages – no more than five. Explain that it is not necessary to draw diagrams that are too detailed – simple drawings are best. Discuss the importance of the labels, especially if measurements or special materials/equipment are required, and how it is vital that the writing is neat and legible.

Discuss with the children why it is important for the pictures and labels to be in the correct order. You could ask, 'What would happen if we carried out this before that?', pointing to the appropriate picture.

Send the children off to draw their own labelled diagrams for one of their methods of joining or strengthening. When they have completed them, ask them to swap their diagrams with another pair and then to carry out the other pair's method.

Plenary

Gather the children together and share some of the diagrams. Compare and contrast them with the model diagram done earlier. Ask for comments about the title and the order.

Ask the children for comments on how easy or difficult it was to draw their own diagrams and to follow other people's diagrams.

Ask them to suggest improvements. You are hoping for positive suggestions, such as extra labels, adding numbers or changing the order.

Tell the children that in the next lesson they are going to look at following instructions in more detail. Ask them to bring in some different examples of instructions from home so that they can share them in the next lesson.

Revving up

Learning objectives

- To sequence instructions in the correct order.
- To follow instructions.
- To identify the key structural and linguistic features of an instruction text.

Resources

- Sheets A and B (pages 61 and 62)
- A collection of instruction texts that the children have brought in from home and some of your own
- A hanging picture board made from following the instructions on Sheet A

What to do

Tell the children that they are going to carry out some more work on writing and following instructions.

Share and talk about the various types of instructions that the children have brought in from home and some of your own. Ask questions such as 'What things do you notice that they have in common?', 'What things are different?', 'Which instructions are the easiest to follow?' and 'Who are they written for?' You are looking for replies that will help you to emphasise the importance of the sequencing and also the purpose and audience for the instructions.

Tell the children that you have prepared some instructions that they are going to follow to make a simple, hanging picture board. Show them your ready-made example.

Writing across the Curriculum

Share an enlarged version of Sheet B. Read the instructions together as a class. What do they notice? (Hopefully that the instructions are not in the correct order!) What do they need to do in order to use the instructions?

Provide each pair with a copy of Sheet B. Ask them to cut up the instructions (or number them) so that they are in the correct order. Give them a short time to do this and then share their results. Agree the correct order (using Sheet A as your guide) together.

Remind them that they will make their own picture frames later and that they will also write some instructions on how to make them. Tell them that in order to help them do this you are going to explain the special features of instruction texts. Share an enlarged version of Sheet A (with the annotations covered up with sticky notes) in order to go through the structural and linguistic features of the text. You can uncover each sticky note as you discuss each point. Ask them what the function of the title is. Ask them to tell you how important it is to have a list of the materials that will be needed and how the numbering helps. Point out the imperative verbs and explain that instructions are written to tell another person what to do. Give some quick examples of the imperative voice, such as 'Keep off the grass', 'Wash your hands' and 'Sit still!' Ask them to suggest others. Emphasise the importance of simple, clear sentences that only contain the information the reader needs – not unnecessary detail.

Finally, ask them to tell you how they think the instructions could be improved (use of labelled diagrams). Ask them to remind you what they learned about drawing and labelling diagrams from the previous lesson.

Give the children the opportunity to make the picture board now or in a D&T lesson.

Plenary

Ask the children to get into small groups to show each other their boards, taking their instructions with them.

Ask them to discuss whether they would change or add to the instructions. They may use coloured felt-tipped pens to revise the instructions if they wish to. Share well thought out alterations with the class.

Set a home task for the next lesson: ask the children to look for examples of freestanding picture/photograph frames at home and to draw a labelled sketch of one.

Explain what 'freestanding' means by comparison with the 'hanging' one they have just made. Remind them to take care with fragile items and to ask an adult whether they are allowed to touch them first.

Display some completed picture boards alongside the enlarged version of Sheet A.

Taking off

Learning objective

- To write instructions.

Resources

- Sheet C (page 63)
- The children's picture frames (made before this lesson)

What to do

Before this lesson, the children need to have made and decorated a freestanding photograph frame. They can use their D&T designs and plans to help them plan and write their instructions.

Tell them that they are now going to write their own set of instructions for making their photo frame. Explain that the instructions need to be written so that someone else could use them to make it. Point out that they need to decide on the main steps of making the frame. The instructions need to be simple and not too detailed, so that a friend, for example, could follow them. What they leave out will be as important as what they put in!

Explain that you are going to start by writing the instructions together as a class. Using an enlarged version of sheet A, revise the important features of instruction writing by using and highlighting the annotations as prompts. Do this as a quick and snappy question-and-answer session.

Now start writing the instructions with the children. Explain that they can use a writing frame to help them later if they wish. Show them an enlarged version of the writing frame (Sheet C).

Share the writing as a class by talking through the thinking and writing process with them. You could start by saying 'What do I need to decide on first? I know – the title. What do instruction titles often start with? That's right – How to…' Ask the children for ideas for a title; for example, **How to make a stand-up photo frame**, and write this in the space on Sheet C. Continue by asking: 'What do we need to add next? That's right – a picture of what the final design looks like. We could draw a sketch or stick a photo here.' Indicate the space on the writing frame.

Remind the children that they can refer back to their plan and picture lists to help them remember the materials and processes which they used. Ask them to look at their D&T plans and notes for a few minutes.

Ask them what they need to decide on next, and point to the 'Materials' subheading on Sheet C. Show them how to present the materials in a list.

Next, ask them to consider what they think the first instruction should be. You could suggest: **Take your piece of backing card and the card frame to go with it, line them up and glue them together around the outside edge.** (Write this on the board.) Ask the children if they think what you have written is too long – is it clear what it means? Ask for their suggestions and rewrite the sentence; for example:

> *1. Put your piece of backing card under your card frame. Carefully line them up.*
>
> *2. Glue around the outside edge of both pieces of card.*

Point out what you have done. 'So instead of one very long sentence and one step I have written three short sentences and split it into two steps. I think it's easier to follow now.'

Go through one more step with the children, using their suggestions and adding and improving the text in the same way as you go. Point out how you are using imperative verbs which tell the reader what to do. Together, read through the instructions you have written.

Provide the children with their own copies of Sheet C and ask them to begin writing. Work with one group of children, helping them choose clear language and to use short simple sentences. Stop the class from time to time and share good examples with them.

Plenary

Gather the children together and ask one child from each group to read out their work. Ask the others to point out the connectives used. Talk about the length of the sentences; check that the imperative is being used. Praise and encourage good use of language.

Have a short discussion session to clarify how instructions differ from other forms of writing. Is it easier to write instructions or to write stories? Which do they prefer? What sorts of books have instructions in them? Who might want to read their instructions? Do instructions describe what you did?

Flying solo

Learning objectives

- To write instructions.
- To edit instructions.

Resource

- Instruction plans from previous lesson

What to do

Tell the children that they are going to finish writing their instructions. Ask them to read through the instructions they have written so far. Tell them to look at their D&T plans and notes again to remind themselves of how they made their frame and the materials they used. Give them a short time to do this.

Ask a child to suggest what their next instruction might be. Write it on the board and use it to illustrate and remind the children how instructions are written. You could ask questions such as *'Is it clear?, Is it easy to understand?, Does it tell the reader what to do?, Shall we number it?, Does it have capital letters and full stops?* and *Can we improve it in any way?'* (For example, by adding an adjective or connective.)

Ask the children to finish writing their instructions. Remind them that it is better to write a few clear, short steps than lots of different complicated steps. Circulate from one group to another and, as before, read good pieces of work aloud from time to time to the rest of the class. Make a point of picking out a good final sentence, using it to illustrate the use of words such as 'finally' or 'last of all'.

When they have finished, ask the children to read through their work quietly to themselves and then ask them to find a response partner. Tell them that they are going to read and check each other's work. Write the following checklist on the board:

1. Read the instructions through together. Is there a 'How to…' title? Is there a heading?

2. Are the instructions in the right order?

3. Are they numbered?

4. Have they used words to link the instructions – such as 'first', 'next', 'then' and 'lastly'? If not, add these in.

5. Do any spellings need checking? Check two words each in a dictionary.

6. Do you think you could make a picture frame by following these instructions?

Talk them through the main points they are looking for when checking each other's work. Circulate and guide the children who need to make changes. Read out some of the revisions, pointing out and praising the salient points of their changes and showing how they have improved their writing.

Plenary

Ask how the response partner session helped them to improve their work. What have they learned about writing instructions? If they were to write a hints sheet for another class, what important points would it include to help these children write successful instructions?

Sheet A

Writing across the Curriculum

(title)

How to make a hanging picture board

(list of materials needed)

Materials
stiff coloured card (A4 or A3)
thin white card
scissors
glue
ruler
sticking tape
pencil, coloured pencils or felt-tipped pens
photographs

(picture to show the reader what they will make)

What to do

(sub heading)

1. Firstly, use a ruler to draw a line around the edge of the coloured card to make a border or frame.

2. Decorate the border using coloured pencils or felt-tipped pens.

(short, simple sentences)

3. After completing the border, draw some rectangles of different sizes on the white card. Use a ruler to do this. Make the rectangles slightly larger than your photographs.

(numbers to show a sequence of steps to follow)

4. Cut out the rectangles.

5. Glue a photo onto each rectangle, leaving a border of white around each photo. You may have to use scissors to trim the photos to fit the rectangles.

(present tense)

6. Arrange the pictures on the stiff coloured card and glue them in place.

7. Cut a piece of string (about 6cm long) to make a hanging loop.

(imperative verb (tells you to do something))

8. Fix the hanging loop to the top of the board at the back. Use sticking tape. Make sure it is securely attached.

PHOTOCOPIABLE

Sheet B

How to make a hanging picture board

What to do

Decorate the border using coloured pencils or felt-tipped pens.

Glue a photo onto each rectangle, leaving a border of white around each photo. You may have to use scissors to trim the photos to fit the rectangles.

Materials

stiff coloured card (A4 or A3)
thin white card
scissors
glue
ruler
sticking tape
pencil, coloured pencils or felt-tipped pens
photographs

Cut out the rectangles.

Fix the hanging loop to the top of the board at the back. Use sticking tape. Make sure it is securely attached.

After completing the border, draw some rectangles of different sizes on the white card. Use a ruler to do this. Make the rectangles slightly larger than your photographs.

Firstly, use a ruler to draw a line around the edge of the coloured card to make a border or frame.

Arrange the pictures on the stiff coloured card and glue them in place.

Cut a piece of string (about 6cm long) to make a hanging loop.

Cut out the rectangles.

Sheet C

Writing across the Curriculum

How to _____

Materials (List the materials you need.)

Picture of final design

What to do
1
2

PHOTOCOPIABLE

Writing Across the Curriculum 63

Chapter 4

Explanation writing

What is an explanation text?
An explanation tells us how something happens or why something happens.

Structural features
- Title to tell the reader what the text will be about
- Usually has an opening statement to set the scene
- A series of logical steps explaining the process
- Often has diagrams

Examples of explanation texts
- write-ups of science experiments
- encyclopaedia entries, text books, non-fiction books

Linguistic features
- Usually present tense (except in historical explanations)
- Third person (impersonal) style
- Uses causal connectives (such as 'because', 'in order to', 'as a result of', 'consequently', 'which means that') to show cause and effect
- Use of time or sequential connectives to aid chronological order (such as 'firstly', 'afterwards', 'meanwhile', 'subsequently', 'finally')
- Often uses the passive
- Technical vocabulary
- Complex sentences

Teaching explanation writing

When children write explanations they have two main hurdles to leap. First, they have to be able to grasp the concept they are trying to explain, which requires some complex thinking skills, and then they have to articulate their understanding in the fairly rigid conventions of the written explanation genre. Plenty of opportunities to speak their explanation before writing will help children to organise their thoughts. Sharing their explanations with response partners at different stages during the writing process will give them a live audience to help them identify 'gaps' in their explanation and reveal specialised vocabulary that has not been clearly defined.

Making flow charts or simple diagrams helps to develop the children's own understanding of the process they are explaining as well as helping the reader understand the text more easily.

Explanation writing – progression

Children are introduced to explanations in Year 2 (Term 2: T17, T19, T20, T21) where they are required to read and make simple flow charts or diagrams that explain a process.

In **Year 3** children develop their note taking skills (Term 1: T20, T21 and Term 2: T17) into making simple records including flowcharts.

In Year 4 the children are introduced to the key structural and linguistic features of a range of explanation texts (Term 2: T20). They are also encouraged to improve the cohesion of their written explanations through the use of paragraphing, link phrases and organisational devices such as sub headings and numbering (Term 2: T24, T25).

In Year 5 children are required to read a range of explanatory texts, noting features of the genre (Term 2: T15), as well as planning and writing their own explanation texts (Term 2: T22).

In Year 6 children read and write explanation texts, focusing on the use of impersonal formal language (Term 3: T15, T16).

Unit 1

Lesson focus
Science Unit 3A – Teeth and eating

Overall aim
To use flow charts and labels to explore ways of recording information and explaining facts. To write a simple explanation poster about why people clean their teeth.

Science emphasis
The children will learn that healthy teeth need healthy gums and that some foods can damage their teeth. They will learn how to keep their teeth and gums healthy.

Literacy link
Year 3, Term 2: T17

About this unit
In this unit, imaginative role play and a talk from a visiting dental health professional will provide background to the children's understanding of dental care. The children will also use information texts, models, posters, videos, and IT resources to broaden their understanding. They will use a variety of simple flow charts and diagrams in order to write a simple explanation.

Switching on

Learning objectives
- To find out about the functions of teeth.
- To role-play a day in the life of a tooth.

Resources
- Sheet A (page 70)
- A large labelled diagram/poster of the parts of a tooth
- Resources about the functions of different types of teeth, such as information books, a video or computer program

What to do
Ask the children to tell you what they already know about teeth. Tell them that over the next few lessons they will be finding out how to look after their teeth and keep them healthy.

Share a labelled picture or poster of a large tooth. Discuss the names and functions of each part. As part of this, explain to the children that their teeth have roots which hold them in place in the jawbone. The gums are soft tissue that surrounds the base of the teeth. Ask them to point to their own gums. Tell them that their gums help to keep their teeth in place and so it is important to keep them healthy by eating healthy foods and including them in their teeth cleaning routine – gentle brushing, not scrubbing! (You could ask your health care professional, in the 'Taking off' session, to discuss and illustrate this in more detail with the children.) Then ask the children to tell you the names of the different types of teeth and their functions. You could use information books, a video or an IT program to support this part of the lesson. Ask the children to put up their hands if they have some second, adult, teeth. Remind all of them that their adult teeth will need to last them for a long, long time.

Ask them if they can identify what sorts of things may damage their teeth. Write their ideas on the board.

Brainstorm ideas of what happens to their teeth throughout the day. Ask questions such as *'What happens to your teeth when you eat your breakfast?'* You are looking for answers that explain that tiny pieces of food get left around the teeth and gums. Some of these little pieces of food will interact with the juices in the mouth to make it acid and this may cause tooth decay.

Explain to the children that they are going to have a role play session about a day in the life of a tooth. Ask them to choose one of their teeth to be the special tooth for the role play. Clear a space in the classroom or go to the hall. Make sure you have a flip chart or board handy.

Challenge the children to visualise their tooth going on a journey through the day: some parts of the day will be dangerous for the tooth, other parts will be safe. Make a game of it. Lead the role play session, going chronologically through each part of the day, from waking to going to bed. Use the ideas on Sheet A to help you invent the journey. You could write each stage of the journey on the board or display an enlarged version of the sheet. Point out the times when they have a meal or a snack or have a drink. Bring these moments to life in the role play; for example: *'Oh dear! A sugary drink is washing all around me; I wish I could rinse it off! I don't want to get little holes in my enamel!'* Take the opportunity to discuss what a better drink or snack would be and use the children's suggestions to carry out the contrasting role play for this; for example, *'Oh, great! He's chosen a glass of water and an apple instead of that awful sticky stuff he likes so much.'*

Plenary

At the end of the session ask the children to tell you some of the good moments of the day for their tooth and some of the danger times. Ask them to explain why.

Write the events and their explanations as bullet points on a flip chart or whiteboard. Give this a title so that it can be put on display.

Revving up

Learning objectives

- To identify some of the linguistic and structural features of an explanation text.
- To draw and label a flow chart.

Resources

- Sheets A and B (pages 70 and 71)
- Bullet point list from 'Switching on'

What to do

Gather the children together and talk about what an explanation is. Tell them that we explain in all sorts of situations throughout the day, often in answer to questions such as 'Why?', 'How?' or 'What happens when?'

Give some simple examples, such as *'I might say to you, "You cannot go out to play at break time today." I would expect you to ask me why and I would say, "Because it is raining." That is a very simple explanation about why I am asking you not to do something.'*

Go through some more simple examples with the children, such as: *"Please bring in your trainers tomorrow.' 'Why?' 'Because we are going to have an outdoor PE lesson.'*

Share an enlarged version of Sheet B (page 71). Ask the children to tell you what the text is about. What question does the text set out to answer? Do they think the text answers this question successfully?

Discuss what makes the text an explanation. These are some of the points which need to be made:

- it answers the question posed in the title;
- it tells you why or how you should do something;

- it explains things or adds to the reader's understanding of what it describes;
- it is written impersonally;
- it is in the present tense;
- it uses clear sentences joined together logically;
- it uses technical terms, such as 'germs';
- it uses simple connectives, such as 'because', 'so' and 'as'.

Tell the children that they are going to write their own explanations later about how to take care of their teeth and in order to help them do this, they are going to make a flow chart. Share an enlarged version of Sheet A and explain why it is called a flow chart. Remind them about the role play they did in the previous lesson about a day in the life of a tooth and tell them that they are going to do a flow chart about this.

Explain that each box in the chart leads on in time order to the next one and shows in diagram form what they worked through in the role play.

Read through the bullet points from the plenary in the last session and talk about when the tooth was in danger and when it was safe.

Model drawing the first three pictures in the boxes with the children. Discuss what was happening and how it affected the tooth. Ask questions such as: *'What was your tooth like when you woke up this morning? Had you remembered to clean him before you went to bed last night? What did you eat for breakfast this morning? Do you think it was good or bad for your tooth?'* Discuss their breakfast choices briefly and their effects on this one tooth. Continue by asking the children: *'Did you brush your teeth this morning? Were you in a hurry? Did your special tooth get brushed well or missed?'*

Tell the children that the drawings need to be labelled in order to make them better understood by the reader. Ask them for suggestions for labels for the first three boxes. For example, you could add the following label to the picture of cleaning teeth after breakfast: 'Clean teeth. Teeth stay clean and safe until next snack.'

Provide the children with their own copy of Sheet A. Ask them to complete each box with a picture of the main things that happen to the tooth during the day. Tell them to add notes and labels to the diagrams in order to explain what is happening to the tooth, and why.

As you move around the classroom, remind the children that the pictures describe what is happening, while the labels should explain or give a reason for it.

Plenary

Share some of the completed flow charts with the whole class, asking for comments and questions.

Ask the children to outline in red the pictures that show the dangerous moments for their tooth and to outline in green the good things that have happened to their tooth.

Taking off

Learning objectives

- To learn about the importance of dental hygiene.
- To devise some questions and record the answers.
- To complete a flow chart.

Resources

- Sheets C and D (pages 72 and 73)
- Ideally, a visit from a dental health professional such as a dental nurse (alternatively, use the hotseating technique with yourself as a dentist)

What to do

Prior to the visit
Prepare the children for the visit of the dental nurse. Have a question-and-answer session asking the children what they think the dental nurse's role is. (You are looking for answers that make the point that she or he works to keep children's and adults' teeth and gums healthy.)

Share an enlarged version of the word bank/glossary (Sheet C). Discuss the meaning of any terms the children are unfamiliar with. Keep the sheet on display for the children to refer to.

Brainstorm what the children think they need to find out about keeping their teeth healthy. Model writing a question on the board, such as: 'Which is the best time to clean my teeth?' Ask the children for two or three other suggestions and write these on the board.

Tell the children to work in pairs to devise a simple list of questions of their own. You are looking for the following sorts of questions: How many times a day should I clean my teeth? How long should I clean my teeth for? What will happen if I forget to clean my teeth? Why is eating sweets bad for my teeth? What is tooth decay? What are fillings?

Share the children's work and as a class decide on the four or five most important questions to ask the dental nurse. Write these questions on a large sheet of paper and put it on display.

Arrange with the dental nurse to agree to a question-and-answer session during her or his visit.

On the day
Proceed with the visit and work with the dental nurse to illustrate and explain how to follow a good teeth cleaning regime.

Use the question-and-answer session as planned. If possible, arrange for another adult to scribe the replies in note form to be used as a group record to allow the children to listen and concentrate.

At the end of the visit, ask the children to write down the answers to the questions. Help them to check their answers against the notes taken by the adult and with the dental nurse.

After the visit
Introduce the children to an enlarged version of Sheet D. Ask them to tell you what it is (a flow chart) and to remind you what a flow chart can be used for. Explain that they are going to use it to explain how to clean teeth correctly.

Go through it step by step, explaining each section. You could say: 'What is the first thing you do when you clean your teeth? You will need to draw a picture in the oval marked '1' and write a label to explain what you are doing.' Model this for them.

Continue to talk them through each step, asking questions such as: 'Now what do you need to do next? Which teeth will you clean first? How do you clean them?' Model another two or three steps for them and remember to show them how to draw up and down arrows to show the direction of the brushing.

Provide the children with their own copy of Sheet D and ask them to fill in their flow chart.

Circulate around the class supporting the children with the task.

Plenary
Ask the children to work in pairs with a response partner. Ask them to check that the sequence of teeth cleaning is correct.

Have a short discussion session. Is this how they actually clean their teeth? What do they need to do differently in order to improve their toothbrushing technique?

Go through the question-and-answer sheet with the class. Have they learned any new or unexpected facts?

Writing across the Curriculum

Flying solo

Learning objective
- To write an explanation text.

Resources
- Sheets C, E and F (pages 72, 74 and 75)
- The completed flow charts from previous lesson
- Paper, felt-tipped pens (to make a poster)

What to do
Tell the children that they are now going to write their own explanation text about how to look after their teeth. Ask them to remind you about the features of an explanation text.

Remind them about the text they shared about washing hands (Sheet B). Tell them that the information from this text has been made into a poster explaining why and how we should wash our hands before we eat. Show them an enlarged version of Sheet E. Point out the way it is laid out. Ask the children about the top line and explain that it is an exclamation, a bold heading, to attract people's attention and make them want to read the poster.

Point out the second sentence. Tell them it is called a statement. You could say, 'This line is rather like a second title. It tells us what the poster is about. It is called a statement. The rest of the poster should explain this sentence.'

Ask them to look at the rest of the poster. Have the writing and pictures successfully explained why we should wash our hands before we eat? Show them how each point leads on to the next one and how the pictures are chosen to add to the meaning. Ask them to tell you how each picture helps the meaning.

Tell the children that they are now going to plan their own explanation poster about how to look after their teeth in a similar way to the poster on Sheet E. Ask them to tell you what things they should do to make sure the poster is easy to read and understand. (You are looking for answers that make the following points: short sentences; not too much writing; set out clearly with one point leading on to another; pictures that help them understand the meaning.)

Provide the children with their own copy of Sheet F. Explain that they are going to use this sheet to plan their poster. Go through each section with them. Explain that it will be used to design their final poster and only needs quick notes and lines and boxes to show where things will go. Tell them that they only need to roughly plan their pictures at this stage; they will draw them properly on the final poster.

Ask the children to work in pairs to plan their poster. Tell them to use their flow charts from previous lessons to help them.

Move around the class, reading out good examples of clear explanations.

Discuss their ideas. Remind them that each piece of writing and each picture should explain the sentence 'Why we need to clean our teeth night and morning.'

When the children have finished planning, gather them together and share some of the poster plans. Share good examples of diagrams, labelling and explanations.

Provide them with a piece of 'best' paper and ask them to use their poster plan to create their final poster.

Plenary
Ask each pair of children to choose another pair to swap posters with and to take it in turns to ask questions and talk about them. Ask them to find one thing that helps to explain something really well and share these comments as a whole class at the end of the session.

Follow-up
Invite a younger class and their teacher in to look at your displays and give them the posters. Ask their teacher if they can be displayed around the infant school. Give the Year 3 children time to read them with the younger children. Make them 'experts' for the session, answering and explaining in response to the younger children's questions.

Sheet A

A day in the life of a tooth

1. Waking up	2. Having breakfast

4. Going to school	3. Being cleaned

5. Playtime	6. Lunch time

8. Drink and snack time	7. Home time

9. Evening meal time	10. Getting ready for bed

Sheet B

Why do we need to wash our hands before eating?

Why do we need to wash our hands before we eat?

Some reasons are obvious.

You can see and sometimes smell the dirt on your hands. For example, maybe your hands are very dirty because you have been playing with dirty things like footballs, sticks, paints or glue, or perhaps you have been mending your bike and have greasy hands. You need to wash your hands after doing these things because you do not want to get the dirt, paint, glue or grease in your food.

Sometimes, your hands will look clean but will still need washing.

This is because our skin comes into contact with little organisms called germs. Some of these germs are good and some of these germs are bad. The bad ones may make us ill, so we need to wash our hands before eating. We do not want to put the germs on our food and then into our mouths as they might make us ill with stomach aches and sickness.

If you have been playing with animals you need to wash your hands, because you may have dust and dirt and germs left on your hands that you cannot see. When you have used the toilet, you can get germs on your hands. So, remember, you should always wash your hands after using the toilet.

The rule for you to remember is: always wash your hands properly before eating.

PHOTOCOPIABLE

Writing Across the Curriculum 71

Sheet C

A glossary of teeth words

Acid	A strong substance that attacks teeth.
Calcium	A substance found in milk and other foods that helps to build teeth and bones.
Canines	The sharp pointed teeth, found on each side of the incisors in humans.
Cavity	A hole in a tooth made by tooth decay.
Crown	The part of the tooth outside the gum.
Dentine	The main yellowish layer of a tooth that is found under the enamel.
Dentist	A person trained to treat teeth.
Enamel	The hard white coating on the outside of a tooth.
Filling	Metal or plastic that is put inside a cavity to fill it and to stop further tooth decay.
Fluoride	A chemical added to toothpaste and sometimes to water to prevent tooth decay. You will find fluoride toothpaste in the shops.
Germs	Tiny living things found all around us. Some cause tooth decay.
Gums	The part of the mouth that holds the teeth.
Incisors	Front teeth used for biting.
Molars	Big chewing (often called double) teeth found at the back of the jaw.
Root	The part of the tooth that grows inside the gum.
Saliva	A liquid inside the mouth that helps us to swallow and digest food.
Tooth decay	When teeth have holes in them.
Toothpaste	A paste used to clean teeth.

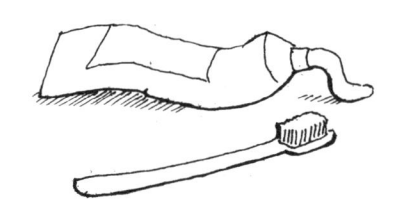

Sheet D

How to clean teeth – an explanation flow chart

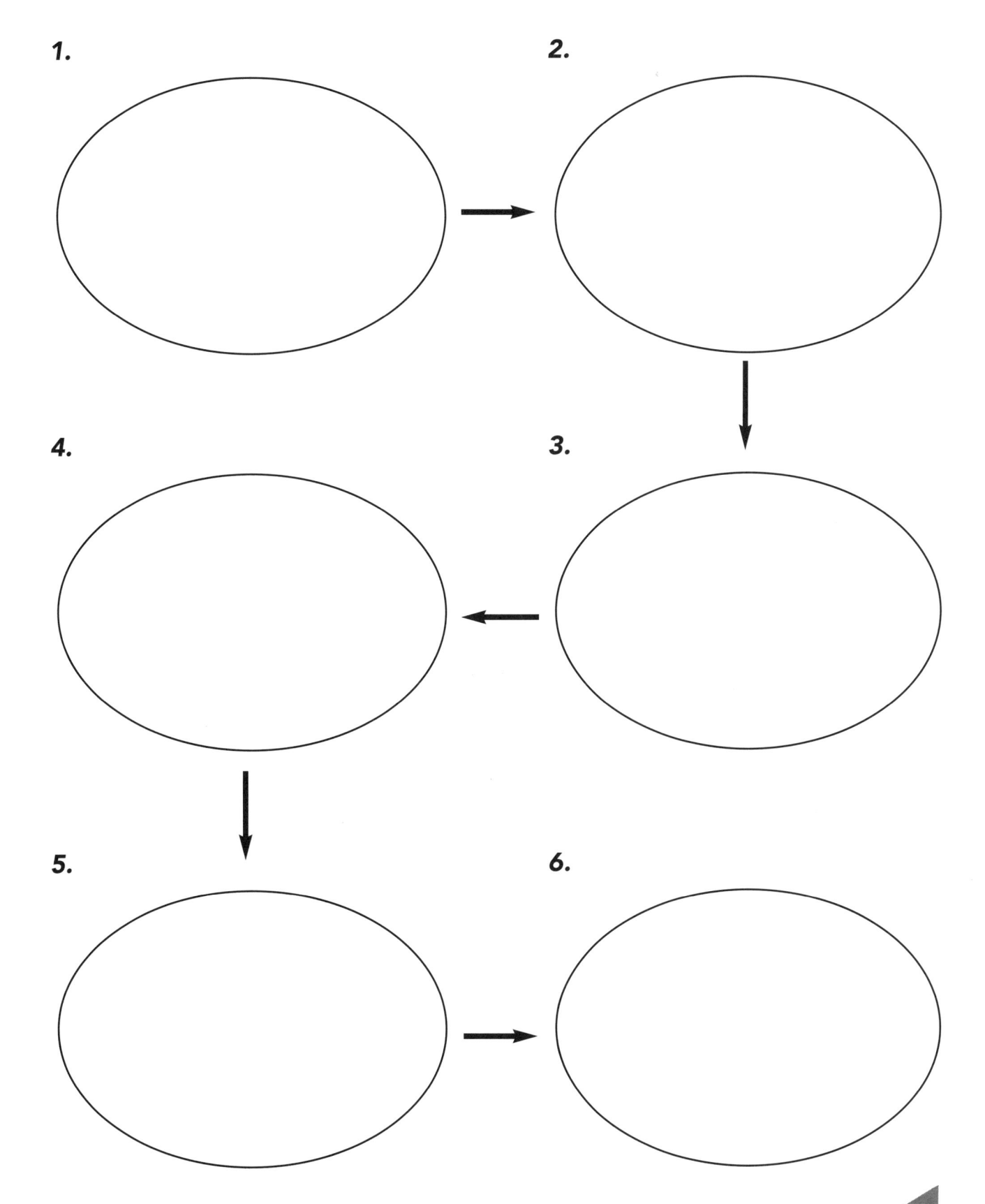

1.

2.

3.

4.

5.

6.

PHOTOCOPIABLE

Writing Across the Curriculum 73

Sheet E

Wash Your Hands Before You Eat!

Why we need to wash our hands before eating ······ opening general statement

Our hands may be covered in all sorts of things.

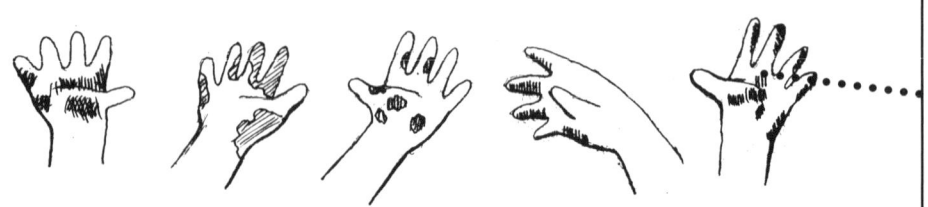

······ first explanation – a simple sentence and pictures

Some of these things will get on our food and may make us ill. Dirt can contain germs that cause illness.

······ second sentence to explain more

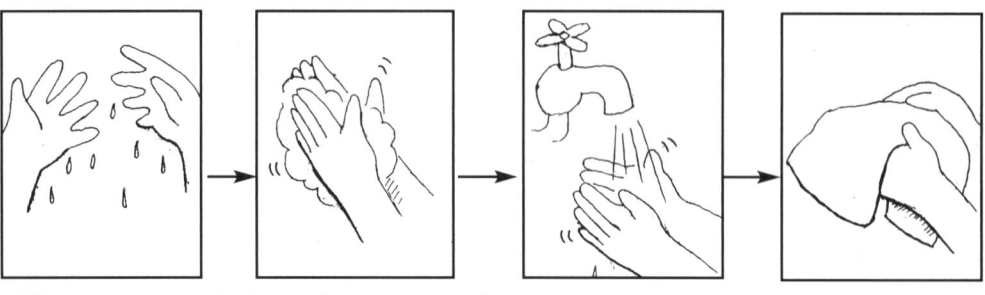

How to wash hands correctly

······ flow diagram and caption to explain how to do it

Remember: you need to wash your hands properly, not just run water over them quickly.

······ further sentence to remind reader what to do

NOW – WASH YOUR HANDS!

HAVE YOU DONE IT WELL? ······ question to check that the message is understood

······ bold title to grab attention

74 Writing Across the Curriculum   PHOTOCOPIABLE

Sheet F

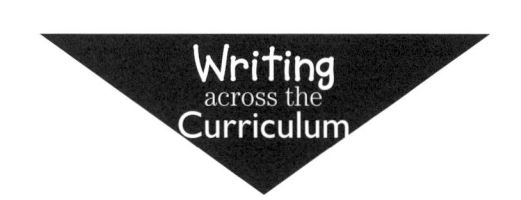

Writing across the Curriculum

Think of a good title. Write it in bold. (Use the one below or think of your own.)

CLEAN YOUR TEETH!

Think of a statement that relates to the title. You can use the one below or make up one of your own.

Why we need to clean our teeth night and morning.

Explain why in short sentences. Add pictures to make your meaning clear.

How to clean your teeth

You can add a small flow diagram here or you can explain in sentences.

What else might you add?

Unit 2

Lesson focus
Citizenship Unit 4 – People who help us – the local police

Overall aim
To identify the features of an explanation text and to write an explanation about the role of the Community Police Officer.

Citizenship emphasis
In this unit the children will meet the officer and ask him or her questions that will help them to understand his or her work in the neighbourhood. They will take notes and write an explanation of his or her role in the community for others in the school.

Literacy links
Year 3, Term 2: T17

About this unit
The children will use question-and-answer sessions to learn what the officer does in his/her work. They will take notes and discuss their findings. They will plan and write a short explanation of the officer's work so that others can understand what the officer's work is in the community. Please note that in some areas there will be a School Liaison Officer who can be approached instead of the Community Police Officer.

Switching on

Learning objectives
- To take notes.
- To write sentences using notes.
- To understand what an explanation is.

Resources
- Sheet A (page 81)
- Books/posters about the work of a police officer
- A3 paper, felt-tipped pens

What to do

Note: it will be necessary before planning this unit to contact the local Community Police Officer or School Liaison Officer in your area to ask him/her to visit your class. Tell him or her that the children are being given the task of explaining the work that the officer does in the community. The officer could explain what he or she does in relation to work in schools; for example, road safety, warning children about strangers, neighbourhood watch – all campaigns that the police support.

Tell the children that they are going to meet their local community police officer who is going to explain the work that he or she does in the community. It is important that the visit is presented in a positive manner as some children may come from backgrounds where they know and are known to the police for a variety of reasons.

Explain that before the officer visits them they are going to think about what a police officer does. Share the books/posters with the children or make the resources available for them to use. Put the children into groups and ask them to brainstorm what they think the job of a police officer is. They should write down the words and phrases that they think show what a police officer does.

Display their brainstorm sheets around the room and ask the groups to look at each other's ideas.

Sit the children in a discussion circle and ask them to tell you what they think the police officer does. You could ask them if they agree with the ideas in the brainstorms. Why do they think we have police officers? What is their work? How do they do their work? List their ideas on a flip chart or board under the heading 'The job of a Community Police Officer'.

Discuss the meaning of the word 'explain'. Tell them that during the next few lessons they are going to gather information together in order to write an explanation of what a police officer does in the community.

Put the children back into their groups and give them their brainstorming sheets back. Ask them to look at their ideas again and to add any other ideas they want to include as a result of their discussion. Then ask them to underline or circle the words and phrases they think are the most important. Explain that these words are called key words and that they provide a summary of the main ideas on their sheet.

Ask children from each group to tell you what their key words and phrases are and note them on the board. Compare each group's notes.

Put the children into pairs and ask them to write two sentences about each point, using the words from the brainstorming sheets and the note taking flip chart. Model how to do this before they begin writing. Ask them to number their sentences in the best order for reading them out.

Plenary

Share some of the sentences. Ask them if they think they have begun to tell (explain) what the police officer does.

Show the children Sheet A and tell them that this is a simple explanation of what a police officer does. Ask them if there are any things on it that they have left out. Point out the title and discuss the order that the explanation points are listed in. Do they think that it is a good order?

Tell them that in the next lesson they will be meeting their local community police officer. Explain that he or she will be telling them about the work they do and that you want them to think of some questions to ask the officer. Ask them to think of some questions under the following headings before the next lesson:

❏ Why there are police officers;

❏ What their job is – how they help us;

❏ What they do in our local community;

❏ What a police station is for.

Revving up

Learning objective

■ To make notes after listening to a talk.

Resources

■ A visitor – a Local Community Police Officer

■ A map of the local area

■ A3 paper

What to do

Introduce the police officer to the children. Point out where the police station is on the map of the area and put a coloured pin on the map to identify it easily.

Ask the officer to tell the children about his or her work. If you have a means of filming or recording the talk, or have an adult who can take notes, it would be useful to do so. It would be helpful to ask the officer to break his or her talk into the following sections and allow the children an opportunity to ask the questions they prepared in the plenary session in 'Switching on'.

At the end of the talk, ask for any further questions and then put the children into their brainstorming groups and give them a sheet of A3 that has three headings on it:

1. Why there are police officers.

2. The job of a police officer – how they help us and the community.

3. What the police station is for.

Tell them that they are going to make notes about what the police officer has told them. Explain that notes are a way of reminding ourselves about the important bits of information that we want to remember. They are written using key words and phrases that help us recall what the speaker said.

Walk around the groups with the police officer and check that the children are putting down the information from the talk. They may write in short sentences but you should encourage them to use brainstorming as a means of making their notes. Give them a few minutes for this task and then ask each group to report back to the class, using their notes. The police officer can help confirm that they are correct.

Put the information the children give you in note form on a flip chart or the board – title it 'The work of PC…' (insert the officer's name). As in the previous lesson, ask the children to use these notes to write two sentences for each point. They could work in pairs to do this.

Plenary

Share some of the sentences. Point out to them that they have written sentences that explain something – they have told us about something in detail.

Tell the children that they are going to use these sentences to write a more detailed explanation and that the officer will be visiting them again to hear and read their explanations.

Taking off

Learning objectives

- To identify the features of an explanation text.
- To plan an explanation.

Resources

- Sheets A and B (pages 81 and 82)
- Brainstorms and sentences from previous lessons

What to do

Ask the children to tell you what they remember about the police officer's visit. Show them the key word list from the previous lesson and ask them if there is anything else they think should be added.

Remind them that they are going to plan an explanation about the work of a police officer in their community and what a police station is for.

Share an enlarged version of Sheet A to remind them what an explanation is. Point out that an explanation needs a title so that we know what is going to be explained and that the title can be a question. Ask them if this question tells the reader what the explanation will be about.

Read the introduction out loud together. Ask them what we learn about the work of a police officer. (Note: 'policeman' and 'policewoman' are not used by the police.)

Read the rest of the explanation to the children. Ask them to identify what the work of a police officer is. Ask them what they notice about the sentences – you want them to recognise that they are mostly written in the present tense. Ask them to look at the words in the explanation. Are there any specialist or technical words? Ask them to identify them and write them on the board.

Writing across the Curriculum

Tell them that the explanation has a conclusion. Ask them to read it out. Is it clear that the explanation is complete?

Remind the children that an explanation is a way of telling people about something or someone clearly. Does the explanation of the work of a police officer help them to remember and understand what the duties of the officer are?

Share an enlarged version of Sheet B. Explain that they can use this sheet to plan their explanation. Remind them to use their notes to help them. Provide each pair with their own copy of Sheet A. Walk around the class giving support where it is needed and read out examples of good explanations being given.

Ask the children to join another pair and read each other's planning sheet. Put the following check questions on the board for the children to refer to:

1. Do you understand the explanation points?
2. Are they in a sensible (logical) order?
3. Do they give you an understanding of the work of the police officer?
4. Do you think they explain what a police station is for?

Ask the children to go back into their pairs and give them time (five to ten minutes) to modify and improve their planned explanation. Check the children's planning and comment on whether you think that they have shown understanding of the police officer's work and what a police station is for.

Plenary

Put the children into pairs and ask them to make up a short quiz about what a police officer does. When they have their questions ready put them into groups of four and ask them to quiz each other. Walk around the groups, checking that the questions and answers help explain the work of a police officer.

Flying solo

Learning objective
- To write an explanation text.

Resource
- Sheet B (page 82) already completed by the children

What to do

Tell the children that today they are going to write their explanation of the work of the local Community Police Officer. Explain that you are going to show them how to use their planning sheets to do this.

Ask them to look at Sheet B. Have they all the information that they think they will need to explain the work of the local police officer in the community? Remind them that they are writing an explanation and need to think about how an explanation is written. Tell them that you are going to model an explanation with them. Ask them how they think you should begin. (You want them to say that you need a title that tells the reader what you are writing about.) Say: *'I think I will write* **What does our local police officer do in our community?'** Explain that making the title into a question helps to make the reader curious and want to know the answer.

You could say that your first paragraph introduces the subject to the reader. Ask for the children's ideas about what you should write as your first sentence. Write down the sentence that tells the reader what is going to be written about; for example: *A police officer's work is to make sure that the laws are kept in our community.*

Tell them that you can now write what the police officer does. *An officer also works with people in the community to help them feel safe.*

Explain that you now want to give more information about the work of the police officer. Ask the children to use their sheet to find information that you can write. As you write their suggestions, ask them to check that you are writing in the correct tense and person.

Remind the children that the explanation has to have a conclusion. You could write: ***The police officer in our community works hard to help us feel safe and to give us advice about what to do if we are worried about crime.***

Ask the children to read the explanation and tell you if it answers the question in the title. Has anything been left out that they think you should include? Can they explain the work of the police officer in the local community after they have read your explanation?

Ask the children to write their own explanation of what a police officer does in the local community. Remind them to put a title and to write an introduction before they give the explanation. Say that you want to see a conclusion at the end of their explanation.

As you walk around the room, read out good examples of explanation sentences and make sure that the children are thinking about the order that they put their points in.

Organise the children into pairs and ask them to check each other's work. Write the check questions from the last session on the board and ask the children to use those as a checking guide. Ask them to tell their partner (politely) if there are any points that could be made clearer.

Give the children time to check their work. Ask them to write their explanation on a piece of paper. They can use coloured pencils and decorate the work when they have completed their writing.

Plenary

Read out some of the children's explanations and show how they are good explanations of the work of the police officer.

If it is possible, arrange for the police officer to arrive at a time when the explanations are complete and on display on the wall. Ask him or her to read them and comment on them. Does the officer think that they explain the work that is done by him or her?

Sheet A

What is the work of a police officer in the local community?

The work of a police officer is to make sure that our laws are kept. The officer also works to make people in the community feel safe.

The police officer tries to prevent crimes from being committed. He or she patrols the streets on foot or in a car. Police officers investigate crimes and try to find evidence that helps to tell the story of what happened, why it happened and who committed the crime.

The person who committed the crime will be arrested and taken to court to answer for his or her actions. The officer will go to court to tell what happened – this is called giving evidence.

Police officers work with different groups in the community to help them keep their community safe. They might work with shopkeepers, schools and local people. They keep the peace at public meetings such as football matches.

The work of the police officer in our local community is to help keep us safe by making sure that people keep the law and to arrest them if they break it.

Sheet B

Writing across the Curriculum

Write at least two sentences for each question.

Remember – you are explaining the work of the Community Police Officer and what a police station is for.

Why are there police officers?

What does a police officer do?

What is the work of the police officer in our community?

What is a police station?

What is the police station used for?

Chapter 5

Letter writing

What is a letter?

A letter is a written message for a particular purpose. It can be informal, such as a letter to a friend or a formal letter when written about business. It can recount an event from the point of view of the writer or can put forward an argument, give information or request action. It is set out in a particular way when sent through the post. Emails are a form of electronic mail that do not follow the rules that handwritten or typed letters do.

Structural features

- Has a specific layout: sender's address in top right-hand corner; date underneath; recipient's address on left-hand side of next line; 'Dear…' (recipient's name) and an ending ('Love from' in informal letters, 'Yours faithfully' or 'Yours sincerely' in formal letters)
- Set out in paragraphs

Linguistic features

- Can be past, present or future tense
- Formal letters use formal and official language (I look forward to receiving a positive reply)
- Informal letters can include slang and colloquialisms
- Usually written in time order
- Written for a specific purpose

Examples of letters

- thank you letters
- job applications
- letters to friends
- school letters to parents
- charity letters asking for donations

Teaching letter writing

When teaching letter writing it is important to ensure that the children are taught to use the correct layout of a letter.

Make sure that they know how to write out their address and the date in full – using numbers does not help to reinforce the spelling of the months of the year.

Encourage the children to identify the audience for their writing. They should plan their ideas and make sure that they are in a sequence that will communicate their message clearly to the recipient of their letter.

Remind the children of the type of writing they are doing – is their letter a recount of an event? Does it put forward a point of view? Is it giving instructions or explaining something?

Introduce the children to the structural features of the different types of letter that they will be writing. Encourage them to identify formal and informal letters and discuss how they use language to convey meaning.

Read different types of letters and ask the children to identify their purpose.

Letter writing – progression

In **Year 3** children are encouraged to write letters for a range of purposes. They are encouraged to write letters that are linked to work in other subjects. They are required to organise letters into simple paragraphs (Term 3: T16, T20, T22, T23).

In Year 4 children are required to identify how and why paragraphs are used to organise and sequence information (Term 2: T19). They learn how to present a point of view in writing, such as a letter (Term 3: T23).

In Year 5 children are encouraged to read and evaluate letters and to consider how they are set out and how the language is used (to gain attention or respect, or to manipulate). They are required to investigate examples of persuasive devices from their reading and to draft and write individual, group or class letters for real purposes, such as to put forward a point of view. They are required to edit the letters and present them in a finished state (Term 3: T12, T15, T17).

In Year 6 they are required to comment critically on the language style and success of non-fiction texts, such as letters (Term 1: T12) and to read and understand examples of official language (Term 2: T17).

Unit 1

Lesson focus
Geography Unit 7 – Weather around the world

Overall aim
To write an informal letter to a friend telling him or her about a holiday they are planning.

Geography emphasis
This unit encourages the children to investigate places where people go on holiday. It invites them to consider places they would like to go to on holiday. They use maps, leaflets and holiday brochures to find information.

Literacy links
Year 3, Term 3: T16, T20, T23

About this unit
This unit encourages the children to use a variety of resources to identify holiday resorts and to find out why people might like to visit them. They will choose a place they would like to visit and investigate what it is like. They will then write a personal letter to a friend telling them about their holiday destination.

Switching on

Learning objectives
- To identify the key features of an informal letter.
- To investigate places that people might go on holiday.

Resources
- Sheet A (page 89) – one copy to put in an envelope and one copy to enlarge
- Brochures, leaflets and information books about holiday destinations in the UK and abroad
- Atlases, world wall map

What to do

Put one copy of Sheet A inside an envelope, addressed to yourself and ask a colleague to bring the letter to you at the beginning of the lesson. (Enlarge the other copy of Sheet A or on an OHT.) Take the letter out of the envelope and tell the children that you have a letter from a friend (or an ex-pupil) telling you about her holiday. Tell the children that you would like to share it with them. Read it out loud.

Ask them to tell you what they remember about it. Can they tell you where they have been on holiday? List the places on the board.

Organise the children into pairs and give them an atlas. Ask them to find two places they have visited and identify them on the wall map of the world with a coloured pin. Some children may not have been on a holiday so ask them to choose a place from the board and find out where it is or think of a place they would like to visit.

Sit the children in a discussion circle and read the letter again. Can they identify the holiday destination on the wall map? Put a pin in the map where the place is.

Show the children the enlarged version of Sheet A. Tell them that they are going to look at the special features of a letter in order to write their own later on. Ask them to tell you what they notice about the layout of the letter. (You want them to tell you that there is an address, a date, a way of starting the letter and a way of ending it. They should identify that it is written in sentences and has paragraphs. You want them to notice that it is written to a friend and ends in a friendly way – 'Lots of love'.) Tell them that the letter is a personal letter. On a flip chart or board, note the aspects of the letter that they identify (to keep for future lessons).

Tell the children that they are now going to find out about holiday places and choose one that they would like to visit. Put them into groups and give them holiday brochures, leaflets and books about places to visit. Make sure they are given information that they can read and understand according to their ability.

Ask the children to choose a destination. Write the following questions on the board and ask them to find the answers for their destination:

- ❏ What is the name of the place you would like to visit?
- ❏ Where is it?
- ❏ What sort of weather does it have?
- ❏ What sort of countryside is there?
- ❏ Is it near the seaside?
- ❏ List three things you can do there.
- ❏ Why have you chosen it?

Ask the children to put a pin in the map to show where the place is.

Plenary

Ask the children to tell each other what they have found out about the place that they would like to visit. Could they find answers to all the questions? Were there difficulties in finding information? How did they overcome them? You want them to report their findings and explain the steps they followed to get their information. Ask them if, after hearing the reports, one place seems more interesting to visit than the others.

Revving up

Learning objective

■ To make notes.

Resources

■ Sheet B (page 90)
■ Brochures, leaflets and information books about holiday destinations in the UK and abroad
■ Notes from the previous lesson

What to do

Tell the children that they are going to think about planning a holiday to the place they investigated in the previous lesson. Ask them to remind you where the places are located and find them again on the wall map.

Tell them to get into their pairs again and check their notes from the previous lesson. Ask them to think about what else they would like to find out about the destination. Give them about ten minutes to check their information and add anything else to their notes.

Share an enlarged version of Sheet B. Explain that they can use this sheet to help them plan a holiday to their destination. Encourage them to use words that are linked to their holiday, such as: leaflets, brochures, maps, weather, climate, hot, dry, cold, wet, journey, transport, destination, distance, leisure, country, continent, location, travel, plane, train, car, walk, plan, suitcase, clothes, tickets, passport, suntan and suntan lotion/cream. You could make a word bank that they could refer to and add to as they work through the lesson.

Before they make their notes ask them to think about the things people need to take with them on holiday. You can list their ideas on the board and discuss which they think will be the most useful. Ask them to list the items that they want to take on their sheet. They could draw the items to see what they would put in the case.

Ask them how they think they could travel to their destination. Note their ideas on the board. Point out that they are using key words and not writing in sentences. Remind them that notes usually consist of key words and short phrases to help us remember things more easily and quickly.

Ask them to think about the items they will need when they travel. Some may have experience of planes, trains and buses; others may not. Discuss what is needed when travelling in this country and abroad to help them appreciate what they are likely to need for this answer.

Walk around the class and check that the children are carrying out the task correctly. Work with one group, perhaps the less able, helping them to locate and record the information they require.

Plenary

Bring in a suitcase and some items or pictures of items that people might take on holiday. Ask the children to tell you what they think you should pack for a holiday to the south of France, using their notes for ideas. Put the items they suggest in the case. When packed, ask them if they think you would have enough for your holiday. They might like to suggest items you would need for a different destination, such as Australia.

Put the children's work on the display board and let them read each other's ideas about the things that they need on holiday.

Taking off

Learning objectives

- To revise the features of an informal letter.
- To write the beginning of a letter.

Resources

- Sheets A and B (pages 89 and 90), already completed by the children, and Sheet C (page 91)

What to do

Remind the children about the letter you had from a friend. Ask them to remind you what it was about. You want them to tell you that the letter was about her holiday plans and what she was hoping to do on her holiday.

Share an enlarged version of Sheet A and tell them that they are going to look in more detail at the layout of the letter in order to be able to write their own. Ask them why they think the writer of a letter puts their own address on it. You want them to tell you that the reader of the letter will know where to send a reply. Ask them if they know their full postal address. Ask them to write it down. (You may prefer not to ask the children to write out their own address but to use the school address instead.) If they are not sure, help them by using their address from the register as a reference for you. Check that they have written their addresses correctly because they will need this as a reference when they write their letters.

Put the children into their pairs and ask them to look at the enlarged version of Sheet A and write down what else they notice about the layout of the letter. Display the notes you made from the first lesson and tell the children they can refer to these if they need to. Give them about five to eight minutes for this task.

Writing across the Curriculum

Share the children's ideas and discuss the following: the letter is written in the first person; it is partly in the future tense and partly in the present tense; it gives information about where the friend is going, the places she is hoping to visit, what she expects the weather to be like and what sort of clothes she hopes to be wearing; it is set out in sentences and paragraphs; it ends with a friendly, informal ending.

Tell the children that they are now going to plan and begin to write their own letter to someone in order to tell them about a holiday they are planning to go on. Explain that they will be using their notes about their holiday destination in order to write the letter.

Show them how to write their letter. Draw the outline of the first page of a letter on the board and show them where you would write your address. Ask *'Should I write the date as well?'* Listen to their responses and then write the date under your address. Write the date in full.

When you have done this, ask the children how they think you should begin the letter. You want them to suggest 'Dear' and the name of your friend. Write this and then say: *'I am going to start my letter with a paragraph beginning under the name of my friend. I am going to tell my friend that I am planning a holiday. Should I write "I am going on holiday" or "I am writing to tell you about my holiday plans"?'* Ask the children to give you a sentence to begin your letter. Write the sentence that they think is best and then ask them how they think you should continue.

Ask them to look at their notes from 'Revving up' – what information do they think you should put next? You want to tell your friend where you are going. How can you use the key words in the notes to do this? Should you use 'I am planning to go' or 'I want to see'? Discuss the tense used. The letter partly uses the future tense. The future uses phrases like 'I will go to'.

Write two more sentences about the holiday that will complete the paragraph. Read it aloud to the children. Is it clear that you are writing about your holiday plans to your friend?

Leave the example on the board and provide each child with a copy of Sheet C. Tell them they can use this to help them write their own letter – to remind themselves how to set the letter out and to help them decide what information they could put into the letter. (For the less able children the sheet can be used to plan their ideas before they write for the more able children it can act as a guide and a reminder of how to set the letter out.)

Walk around the room and check the children's work. Read out good sentences. You could work with those children who need your help to ensure that they are writing in sentences that are in the correct tense.

Plenary

Ask the children to read out the beginnings of their letters. Have they introduced the idea that they are planning to go on holiday? Have they set out their letters correctly? Do they have their address on the top right-hand side of the page, the date underneath it and the letter beginning with 'Dear' and the friend's name?

Tell the children that they will complete their letter in the next lesson.

Flying solo

Learning objective

- To complete a personal letter.

Resource

- The children's letter beginnings from the previous lesson

What to do

Tell the children that they are going to complete their letters today. Explain that you are going to show them how to do this. Remind them how the letter was set out in the last lesson. Write the beginning of the letter on the board and ask the children what they think you should write next. Tell them that they can use their letter planning sheet to help them. Say *'I am going to tell my friend what the place is like that I am planning to visit. I think I will start the next paragraph by writing:* **The place I am** *going to is called ... It is in* (name of country).' Ask the children to tell you what to write next. Do they want you to mention the weather or what you can do there? Write down the sentences they suggest and read the paragraph. Do they think it makes sense? Does it give your friend interesting information about your holiday plans?

Write the last paragraph in the same way, asking the children what they think you should tell your friend about, what you will need to take with you and how you will get there. Write down the sentences they suggest. Say you want to invite the friend to come with you and write *I would like you to come with me on my holiday. I think that we will enjoy ourselves visiting the different places I have mentioned to you. Please come with me.* Ask them if they think they can improve your ideas.

Remind them to end the letter informally and sign their first name clearly so that their friend knows who the letter is from. Show them how to do this by writing the ending of the letter on the board.

Tell the children to complete writing their letter. Remind them to write in paragraphs and to use Sheet C to help them if they want. Walk around the classroom and check that the children understand the task and can complete it. Help the children who find the task difficult.

Ask the children to read each other's letters and check that the addresses, dates and greetings are written correctly.

Plenary

Ask the children to tell you what they have learned about the different holiday destinations after reading the letters. Did they find the letters interesting? What sorts of things did they enjoy reading about?

Finally, ask the children to remind you what type of letter they have written. Ask them to tell you what an informal letter is and when they can write one.

Sheet A

21 Handy Road
Calton
Newtown
N02 3LY

10 August 2004

Dear

I am writing to tell you about the fantastic holiday I am planning to go on in France. I want to go to Paris, which is the capital of France. There are a lot of exciting places to visit and enjoy. I shall stay in a small hotel on the West Bank of Paris. The hotel has a restaurant that serves good food that I will enjoy.

First, I will go to see the Eiffel Tower and next I will visit the Louvre. I shall enjoy looking at the paintings. I know about a little café that serves good coffee so I will have coffee and cakes. Each day I will do something different. I want to plan a trip on a boat on the river and I want to visit the shops.

The weather should be hot and sunny so I will be able to wear my new holiday clothes without a coat. The city of Paris is a good place to visit and I hope to go again to see the things I might miss on my first visit.

How are you? I hope that you are well and enjoying teaching your class. I expect that they are very good pupils.

Take care of yourself. I will come and see you soon.

Lots of love

Shelagh

Sheet B

Writing across the Curriculum

Things I might need on holiday

Think about the items you might take on holiday – suitcase, clothes, sunglasses, suncream and other items. What do you think that you will need?

List the items here:

Travelling to my holiday

Think about the things you need when you travel, such as tickets, money and passport.

List the items you think you will need to be able to travel here:

Sheet C

Writing across the Curriculum

Write your address under here:

Write the date in full under here:

Who are you writing to?

Start with 'Dear' and the name:

_____

Think about how you will start your letter.

Explain that you are going on holiday and say where you are going.
Use phrases like: I am planning to go, I will take, I want to visit

Tell your friend about the holiday place. Which country is it in?
What will the weather be like? What can you do there?

Tell your friend what you will need to take with you. How will you get there?

Ask your friend to come with you and end your letter – remember to write only your first name at the end as this is a personal letter to a friend who knows you.

PHOTOCOPIABLE

Unit 2

Lesson focus
Citizenship Unit 9 – Respect for property

Literacy links
Year 3, Term 3: T16, T20, T23

Overall aim
To write a formal letter to the headteacher with suggestions for making improvements to the school's litter problems.

About this unit
This unit encourages the children to investigate their own school in order to find out how the environment can be improved. They will find out how to write a formal letter in order to write to their headteacher suggesting ways that any litter problems in the school can be improved.

Citizenship emphasis
This unit encourages the children to investigate the litter situation in their school and to make suggestions for how it can be improved. They will discuss why it is important for the school community to take care of their school.

Switching on

Learning objectives
- To make notes after listening to a talk.
- To discuss the litter situation in their school.

Resources
- Sheet A (page 97)
- A visitor – the school's site manager, caretaker or cleaner – someone who can talk about how litter is managed in the school
- A3 paper and felt-tipped pens

What to do
Before the lesson, put a copy of Sheet A into an envelope addressed to your class and arrange for the school secretary to bring it in to you. (To make it more realistic, alter the details on the sheet to match your school's address, class name, and the headteacher's name. You can also alter the date.)

You will also need to arrange for the site manager/caretaker/cleaner to visit your class for this lesson.

Read the letter to the class and discuss its content. Do they think that there is a litter problem in the school? Record their responses on the board.

Tell them that you have arranged for the site manager (caretaker/cleaner) to visit them to explain how the litter in the school is currently dealt with. Tell them they will need to listen carefully because they are going to make notes after the talk.

Sit the children in a discussion circle and ask the visitor to tell them how the school is kept litter free. Take notes during the talk to remind you what was said. Encourage the children to ask questions after the talk. You could write some questions on the board to start them off. For example:

- ❏ Is the school easy to keep tidy?
- ❏ Do children drop litter and make a mess?
- ❏ Are the classrooms looked after properly?
- ❏ Does our class keep our room tidy? Where is litter dropped?
- ❏ Whose responsibility is it to help keep the school clean?
- ❏ How can the pupils help to keep the school tidy?
- ❏ How can everyone ensure the problem is dealt with successfully?

Organise the children into groups and give each group a piece of A3 paper and some felt-tipped pens. Tell them that you want them to make notes about the discussion they just had. Remind them that notes are made using key words and phrases and that is what they need to do when they are doing their brainstorm.

Tell them the purpose of their notes is to identify the main points that the visitor made. Suggest that they could divide the page into two columns with the headings 'good' and 'bad' at the top and list the points made under the correct heading. Remind them that they are only writing notes – they do not have to write complete sentences – they could use abbreviations, single words and short phrases.

Go around the groups with the visitor and talk to the children to check that they understand the task and are putting their points down.

When complete, display their brainstorms around the classroom and tell the children to go around the class and read each other's ideas.

Then ask each group to stand near their brainstorm and tell you what they have put down about the talk. List the different points they make on a flip chart or the board, under the heading 'The litter situation in our school'.

Ask the children to tell you which they think is the most important point, the next point and so on and number them. Read them back in order to the children – do they think that their points summarise the site visitor's talk? Does the visitor think that they have got all the points he or she made?

Plenary

Ask the children to sit in the discussion circle. Do they think it is important to keep the school tidy and, if so, why? Note their comments on a flip chart entitled 'Our responsibilities in school'. Ask them to think about what happens when the school is not kept tidy and note their responses.

Revving up

Learning objective
- To understand the key features of a formal letter.

Resources
- Sheet A (page 97)
- Some examples of formal letters

What to do

Remind the children about the headteacher's letter they read in the previous lesson. Tell them that they are going to reply to this letter and in order to do that they need to learn about how to set out a formal letter correctly. Ask them to tell you how they think the headteacher's letter might differ from a letter they might receive themselves from a friend or a close family member. Would the layout be the same? Would the words used be different? In what ways? How might the beginning and ending of the letter be different? Write their ideas on the board or flip chart.

Show the children the selection of formal letters you have gathered. Share relevant details, such as how the addresses are set out, how they begin and end, and the type of words and phrases used in them. Are they all handwritten? Do the children think all formal letters will be handwritten or typed? Explain that the letters are formal ones; they are written for a particular purpose – to inform, enquire, complain, persuade or congratulate, for example.

Share an enlarged version of Sheet A again. Explain that, although the headteacher knows them all, he or she has written a formal letter addressed to the class as a whole and that it is a serious letter, asking them to carry out a particular task for a specific purpose.

Go through all the features of the letter and annotate it as you go. Points to consider include:

- the sender's address in the top right-hand corner, the date underneath;
- the recipient's address on the left-hand side of the next line;
- Dear (Sir, Madam or their name if known);
- opening paragraphs to state the reason for writing;
- further paragraph to give the details in a logical order;
- a final paragraph to make clear the action required;
- a formal ending ('Yours faithfully' if recipient's name is unknown or 'Yours sincerely' if it is known).

Underline words and phrases in the letter that indicate the use of formal language, such as 'I am writing to…', 'I am concerned about…', 'It is important that…' and so on. Point out that the letter is trying to persuade them to do something: 'I hope that you agree with this idea,' and 'I am writing to ask for your help…' Explain that the letter also expects them to respond: 'I look forward to reading your letters…'

Tell the children that they are going to read the sample letters you have shown them and underline examples of formal language. They should look for phrases discussed earlier, such as 'I am writing to' and 'I would like your support/help/assistance'. Ask them to identify who is sending the letter and what the purpose of the letter is.

Ask the children to read out the examples of formal phrases that they have found. Do the others agree that they are formal phrases? Read out some of the letters and ask the children to tell you what they are about. Do the others agree?

Plenary

Sit the children in a discussion circle. What do they think about the headteacher's letter? How should they respond to it? List their ideas and explain the idea of a survey before the next lesson.

Ask them to remind you what sort of letter the headteacher sent. How can they tell that it is a formal letter? List their responses on a flip chart that they can use for future reference.

Before the next lesson, ask the children to carry out a survey of the school to find out about the litter situation.

Put them into mixed ability groups and give each group a task to complete. One group could survey the school to check how many litter bins there are and where they are. Another group could check where litter is dropped around the school grounds. A third group could photograph the litter, using a digital camera. A more able group (as an extension task) could draw a plan of the school for the other groups to put their findings on. They could show where the litter bins are and where there is litter dropped. Allow about 20 minutes for the survey and ask them to make notes of their findings.

Share the results and ask the children if they think there is a litter problem in their school. If so, ask them to share ideas about how this can be solved. Note their ideas on a flip chart with the title 'Improving the litter situation'. The ideas could be presented as a chart with one column listing the problems and another column listing how these could be solved. Display the ideas so that the children can refer to them later.

Taking off

Learning objective

■ To plan a formal letter.

Resource

■ Sheet B (page 98)

What to do

Tell the children that today they are going to use the information they found from the litter survey to plan their letter to the headteacher. Show them an enlarged version of Sheet B and tell them that they can use this to plan their letter. Explain that you are going to show them how to do the planning.

Ask them to remind you what a formal letter is. Say *'I am going to write a formal reply to the headteacher about our ideas to help solve the litter problem in school. What do you think I should put first?'*

Write the addresses on the letter, commenting, *'I am putting my address on the right-hand side of the letter and the name and address of the headteacher on the left.'* Ask if you have left anything out. You want the children to remind you about writing the date under your address.

Begin to write the first paragraph of the letter. Remember to model gathering your ideas and rehearse an opening sentence. Write **I am writing in reply to your letter about the litter problem in school.** Do the children think this is a good start. What else can they suggest that you write?

Tell them that you are now going to write a couple of sentences explaining the results of the survey. Say *'First I must tell the headteacher that we conducted a survey. I could write:* **Our class has conducted a litter survey to find out what the litter problems in the school are.** *I could then write:* **We have discussed our results and think that there are ways we could make the litter situation improve.***'*

Ask the children if they can give you ideas about what should come next. You may decide to list the ideas that you have to improve the litter situation and ask the children to give you a sentence explaining what can be done about each problem they found in their survey.

Ask the children to work in their groups on a particular problem and give you the sentence(s) that they think will explain their ideas to the headteacher. They could read their sentences to another group to check that they make sense and make any changes necessary.

Write the sentences on the board, read them aloud and suggest any changes you think are necessary.

Finally, say *'I must finish the letter. As it is a formal letter and as I know the headteacher's name, I will write* **Yours sincerely** *and sign my name.'* Read the letter again and ask them if they think it answers the letter that they were sent.

Tell the children they are now going to work in groups to plan their own letter to the headteacher which they will write in the next lesson. Give them copies of Sheet B to use as a reminder of the layout and to plan their letter. They could fill in their addresses and the date straightaway. They should work in their groups to discuss their ideas – each group could work on the results of the survey that they did.

Tell them to think about the following:

❏ How will they begin their letter? They should write their sentences on the sheet.

❏ What will be the order of the ideas they have? Which points will they want to put first?

❏ How will they end their letter? Do they want the headteacher to agree with their ideas?

While the children are doing their planning, check each group's work and make sure that they are using Sheet B correctly. You could time each section of the planning to make sure that all the sections are completed.

Plenary

Ask the children to work with a response partner and check that they have written the addresses correctly, put in the date and put down their ideas for each part of the letter. Remind them that the letter should be written in the first person and use formal (serious) sentences.

Look again at the letter you wrote on the board and any other work, such as their surveys, that you have displayed.

Finally, ask each pair to come up with a catchphrase that will remind people to put their litter in bins. The class could display the catchphrases around the school to remind their peers to think about what they should do with their litter.

Flying solo

Learning objective
■ To write a formal letter.

Resources
■ Sheet B (page 98) already completed by the children
■ Visitor from 'Switching on' lesson

What to do

Arrange for the visitor from the 'Switching on' lesson to visit the class to hear their ideas and comment on them before they begin to write their final letter to the headteacher.

Sit the children in their discussion circle and ask them to tell the visitor about their ideas on the litter situation and how to improve it as part of their contribution to the school community. After they have heard his or her comments, the children should be able to modify their letter plans if they need to. Allow about 15 minutes for this discussion.

Remind the children about the sample letter that was completed in the last session. Read it out again and discuss the layout and use of language in it.

Ask them to tell you about the layout and language used in a formal letter. (You want them to tell you about the two addresses, the use of paragraphs and that the letter is written in the first person. You want them to tell you that it is a formal piece of writing written about a serious topic.)

Set the children the task of writing their final draft. They could write their letter on writing paper or word process it. Walk around the classroom helping the children with their writing and offering support to those who need it. Give the children about 20 minutes to half an hour to do the draft.

Put them in pairs and ask them to check each other's work. Are the letters set out properly? Do they have both addresses? Are they written in the first person? Are there paragraphs? Put the questions on the board for the children to use as checking guides. Go round the pairs and help them with their checking. Allow no more than ten minutes for this task.

Ask the children to edit their work and to write their final letter.

Walk round the class and read out good examples of the letter. Give the letters to the headteacher when they are completed.

Plenary

Ask the children to work in their groups and prepare ideas for an assembly that explains how the pupils in the school can improve the litter situation. The assembly could be developed and presented as a means of allowing the children to play a role in identifying that they have a responsibility to help keep the school site tidy.

Sheet A

Writing across the Curriculum

Mayberry Primary School
Ashton Avenue
Mayberry
MA1 2RY

10 June 2004

Class 3
Mayberry Primary School
Ashton Avenue
Mayberry
MA1 2RY

Dear Class 3

I am writing to tell you that I am concerned about the litter situation in the school. There seems to be an increase in litter around the school site. It is important that the school community keeps the school tidy and free of litter.

The governors and I think that it is the responsibility of all the people in the school to keep it clean and litter free. I hope that you agree with this idea. I would like you to investigate the litter situation in the school and let me know in a letter how you think things can be improved and the school kept tidy and clean.

I am writing to ask for your help because I know that you are a good class and will be able to help with some good ideas. I look forward to reading your letters when you have finished your investigation into the school litter situation.

Yours sincerely

John Smith

John Smith
Headteacher

Sheet B

Writing across the Curriculum

Plan your letter using the hints below.

Write your address under here:

Write the date in full under here:

Who are you writing to?
Write their name and address below:

Start with 'Dear' and the name:

Think about how you will start your letter:
Explain that you are replying to the headteacher's letter about improving the school litter problem. Write two or three sentences for this paragraph.

For your next paragraph write about the ideas you have to improve the litter situation.

End your letter. Write your first name and surname as this is a formal letter.

Yours sincerely